CONTENTS

CONTENTS

CONTENTS

Discovery

People discovered Scandinavia and Finland about seven thousand years ago. Before that a great sheet of ice had covered northern Europe for more than 20,000 years.

Scandinavia appears on a map from the second century by the Greek-Egyptian geographer Claudius Ptolemaeus. He thought it was a small island north of Denmark.

The Vikings were better informed, and their travels expanded world awareness about the Nordic area.

After the Second World War, Finland was remembered in the west as the country that had defied the Red Army. Yet it was seen by the east as a reliable friend.

Reputations wax and wane, whether for music, paper, ships, design or sport. Today Finland stands out for its technology, which has moved it from the periphery to a place in the centre of Europe.

1.1. WHY DON'T FINNS USE THE NAME FINLAND?

The word comes from Greek and Latin (Fennia), although how that started is unsure. When Roman writers referred to the Fenni they were talking about nomadic Lapps, and the same is true about "Finns" in Norse sagas. The confusion was because Finland didn't exist as a political and social entity then.

The Germany geographer Hartman Schedel put the label Finland on the whole place in 1493 and it stuck. The Finnish language has a different word for the country, "Suomi", which also means the Finnish language. To complete the paradox, this word has its origins in Sami, the language of the Lapps.

1.2. ISN'T IT A DISADVANTAGE TO HAVE SUCH A REMOTE LOCATION?

It was in the past, when foreign goods tended to be much more expensive and Finnish products could not easily compete on distant markets. On the other hand, it can be nice to be off the beaten track. Central areas suffer more from meddling foreigners and marauding armies.

More recently, Finland has gained greatly from "death of distance". In a networked world it makes no practical difference whether communications take place over one kilometre or ten thousand. The periphery is where the network ends, whereas Finland has a denser electronic communications net than anywhere else.

1.3. WHAT CAN YOU FIND IN FINLAND AND NOWHERE ELSE?

Where souvenirs are concerned, Lapp hats have minimal utility elsewhere, glassware is a matter of taste and reindeer skins moult if you do more than look at them. For personal experiences, you'll never see a city street outside Finland where so many people are using a cell phone, but the rest of the world is catching up.

On the other hand, other countries do still have unspoilt countryside, sunlit summer nights, vast empty snowy hills, beautiful lakes and islands, clean cities, open roads, peace and quiet. But these things are getting rarer all the time.

1.4. WHAT MAKES FINNISH PEOPLE HAPPY?

Assuming that people tell the truth, spiritual and personal values count for more than material assets. A survey in Seura magazine in 1999 put "home sweet home" at the top of the list. Then came "sunny weather". An "honest relationship" was number three and a "trusting relationship" number four. Five was "the freedom to be oneself" and six was "a freshly cleaned home".

The first material pleasure was right down at number 19: "More money in my bank account than I remembered".

Geography

Finland is in the north of Europe, with Russia to its east and Sweden to its west.

Its total land area is about 340,000 square kilometres. This makes it the fifth largest country in the European Union, after France, Spain, Sweden and Germany.

65% of the country is covered with forest and 10% is under water. There are about 188,000 lakes. The largest, Saimaa, covers 4,400 square kilometres.

The bedrock is granite, from the Precambrian period. Soil cover is thin. The landscape is fairly flat, rising only an average 152 metres above sea level. The only mountainous area is in the northwest, where the tallest peak, Halti, rises 1328 metres.

2.1. WHY ARE THERE SO MANY LAKES BUT SO FEW HILLS?

The part of the earth now called Finland was once very mountainous, though there was no one around to see it. The granite bedrock is the base of range of mountains created when the earth's crust was formed, but six hundred million years of erosion have cut them down to size.

These hills were then planed flat and smooth by ice ages, when glaciers pushed away the soil. When the thick ice sheet melted, water filled up the dimpled bits.

2.2. WHY AREN'T FINNISH CLOCKS ON THE SAME TIME AS WESTERN EUROPE?

People identify Finland with Scandinavia and so think of it as part of western Europe. Politically and economically it is, but geographically it is a long way to the east. Helsinki falls on a line of longitude between Athens and Istanbul.

It's a trip of 1500 kilometres to Brussels but only 900 kilometres to Moscow. So it makes sense for Finland to be in a time zone one hour ahead of western Europe.

2.3. WHY DO FINNS SAY THEY ARE NORDICS BUT NOT SCANDINAVIANS?

Scandinavia is a geographical area and a linguistic area. In terms of its geography Finland is not part of the Scandinavian peninsular and its language is very different from Swedish, Norwegian or Danish.

Racially, the Finns are Nordic. The word also describes the historical and cultural heritage that Finland shares with its neighbours in the north of Europe. Not that Finns mind being called Scandinavians. It's a positive thing.

2.4. WHAT IS DIFFERENT ABOUT LAPLAND?

Everything. A third of Finland is north of the Arctic Circle and most of it is Finnish Lapland. This is tundra, vast flat nearly treeless plains. The winters are fierce and the land is poor. For the indigenous inhabitants, who like to be called Sami rather than Lapps, reindeer herding has been the main source of income, though services are increasingly important.

There are just 4000 Finnish Sami but there are far more Sami in Swedish and Norwegian Laplands.

3.1. WHAT CLOTHES SHOULD I BRING ON A VISIT TO FINLAND?

The early summer can be pleasant but it's not reliably warm till June. A raincoat and umbrella make good sense all the time if you plan to spend time outdoors. After September in central Finland, and after October in the south, it can be snowy and cold. You'll need a warm and windproof jacket, a hat that covers your ears, gloves and lined shoes with thick, non-slip soles.

Clothes and footwear suitable for a Finnish winter are just not available in many southerly countries, so buy them after you arrive. But if you're here for a just meeting, you'll find buildings are so well heated that normal summer indoor clothes are comfortable all year round.

3.2. ARE VERY LOW WINTER TEMPERATURES DANGEROUS?

For obvious reasons there are not a lot of people living on Finland's winter streets. Those that do are generally beyond caring about health hazards. If you dress properly, though, the winter is no risk to health, and a walk on a sub-zero but bright day can be invigorating.

Winter clothes must include a hood or hat, because your body can lose so much heat via the top of your head. When it's very cold, or with a strong sub-zero wind, you should also cover your forehead, cheeks and chin, because the skin on them can freeze. This is not life-threatening but it stings when it thaws.

3.3. WHERE IS THE BEST PLACE FOR GOOD WEATHER IN SUMMER?

In early summer, the Åland Islands get more sunshine and less rain than any other part of Finland. The nearby Turku archipelago also gets better weather than the mainland then. In July the warmest place is usually the Salpausselkä ridge that sweeps across southern Finland through Lahti and Lappeenranta.

The second half of July is generally the hottest part of summer, but there is also the greatest chance of thundershowers. Mellower weather follows in August, when Savonlinna, Kuopio and Joensuu, in Finnish lakeland, tend to be the warmest places. Also lake water temperatures are then often above 20°C.

4.1. WHAT CAUSES THE MIDNIGHT SUN AND POLAR NIGHT?

The earth spins as it orbits around the sun, but the axis of spin and the plane of orbit are not at right angles to each other. Instead the earth is spinning at a tilt of 23.5°. It is because of this tilt that there is a difference in the length of days in summer and winter. The closer you get to the poles, the greater the difference is.

At the far north, or far south, summer nights and winter days shrink down to nothing. This phenomenon defines the Arctic (or Antarctic) Circle: the border within which it occurs. In fact, the angle of tilt is decreasing, so the Arctic Circle is moving farther north, 14.4 metres a year.

4.2. HOW CAN YOU SLEEP IN SUMMER OR DO ANYTHING IN WINTER?

Many people do sleep less in the summer, without feeling the worse for it. The "winter blues" are less fun. SAD (Seasonal Affective Disorder) is said to affect up to one in five people living in northern latitudes when the days become dark. Its symptoms are depression, lethargy, lack of concentration, craving for sugar, difficulty in waking up in the morning and irritability.

The brain produces a different set of mood-altering chemicals when the eyes receive less light. Ordinary lighting is not enough to compensate. The traditional Finnish treatment used to be a package holiday to the Canary Islands. A more lasting alternative is 10-30 minutes a day of light therapy with special lamps that are ten to twenty times brighter than room lamps.

4.3. WHAT ARE THE NORTHERN LIGHTS?

The aurora borealis, as the Northern Lights are also known, looks like a flapping curtain in the sky or points radiating from a single dot. Its colours are white, yellow, green and red. The phenomenon is quite unpredictable and can be seen only against a clear, dark night sky. It is more common in winter months above the arctic circle but is sometimes seen farther south.

The northern lights are caused by particles emitted by the sun. Most of these are forced round the earth by its magnetic field but some penetrate into the atmosphere along the lines of the field in polar areas. When they meet air molecules in the atmosphere, at a height of about 100 kilometres, they create flickering bursts or sheets of light.

4.4. ISN'T THE GREENHOUSE EFFECT GOING TO BE GOOD FOR FINLAND?

No one knows what a warmer climate would do to the patterns of rainfall, wind, etc., so it wouldn't necessarily make Finland into an earthly paradise. Obviously the effects wouldn't be as catastrophic as in some areas but, even in the north, warmer doesn't automatically necessarily mean better. For one thing a thinner ozone layer will have more impact in the north.

Also a warmer climate will not suit Finland's flora and fauna, which have adapted to present conditions. There will be more plant diseases and pestilence, which is now kept in check by the harsh winter. And, if the sea level rises, there will be flooding on the low-lying west coast.

Environment

More than 200 000 square kilometres of Finland is covered by trees. This is two-thirds of its total area.

The forest cover extends for more than 1000 km from south to north. Farmlands are few and concentrated in the south. Most nature reserves are in the north of the country. 2.6 percent of the country's total productive forestland is under protection.

More land is under water than under the plough. Lakes cover 33,500 square kilometres. There are also extensive wetlands, although many were drained and converted to forestland.

Water pollution by industry and cities has been cut drastically but the load from agriculture has not. Most atmospheric pollution is not Finnish in origin but arrives on the winds from Russia and Estonia.

5.1. WHY DON'T THE FINNS STOP CUTTING DOWN TREES?

Why should they? Resource inventories show that there is more wood growing in Finnish forests than ever before, so trees are not being felled at an unsustainable rate. Thinning is a part of forestry. Any forest that is clear cut is replanted.

Finland doesn't have primeval forests like Canada. Practically all forestland has been exploited by man for centuries. The abundance of waterways means that nothing has been inaccessible. So there are no virgin forests, even within conservation areas. But clear-cutting is going out of fashion, if only because it looks so ugly.

5.2. CAN'T MAN'S IMPACT ON THE FORESTS BE REDUCED?

About two-thirds of woodland is privately owned, where the average forest size is just 31 hectares. That means a lot of owners. The constitution contains strong guarantees of property rights, but an increasing number of forest owners live in towns and their attitude towards their land is becoming more sentimental. The farmers that used to own most forestland saw it as just a source of winter income and employment.

Forest management plans that provide more diversity are gaining ground. Meanwhile on state-owned land, completely unexploited areas are being established, where man's impact will eventually disappear. The main problem is forest fire. Fires are a natural part of the forest ecology that shouldn't be prevented but can't be allowed to spread to other areas.

5.3. ISN'T A PAPER MILL INCOMPATIBLE WITH A CLEAN ENVIRONMENT?

In terms of pollution, the forest industry has made good progress. Paper mills still smell odd but that's because the compound in question is smelly at such low concentrations. A more serious problem is the particles that they used to discharge into lakes and rivers. Effluent is now minimal and papermakers are getting close to a completely closed process, where all water will be recycled and nothing discharged.

The main menace to the water now comes from acid rain, and from farmers who use excess fertilizers and take inadequate precautions to prevent run-off.

5.4. ARE THINGS IN BETTER OR WORSE SHAPE THAN BEFORE?

The state of the Gulf of Finland is deteriorating because it receives an extra 7 000 tonnes of phosphates and 120,000 tonnes of nitrates every year. Finland and Estonia can influence this a bit but there will be no decisive change before Russia does something about effluent from St. Petersburg. Inland the situation is better. Emissions by municipalities and industry have fallen. Most Finnish lakes are still pure although there is still air pollution, mostly from abroad, so acid rain continues.

A recent improvement is the restoration of watercourses to their original condition. Rapids were cleared and straightened in the last century to allow logs to be floated down them. Now that the forest industry is supplied by road, the rivers can be reconstructed, making them more beautiful for man and friendlier for fish.

Wildlife

Finland has over 40,000 species of fauna and flora. Among the vertebrates the biggest group are birds, some 360 species. The number of birds of prey is declining and they need protection but the whooper swan, Finland's national bird, now breeds in more areas than before.

There are about 70 mammal species, the most widespread being the fox, weasel and hare. In addition to the reindeer, which is domesticated, the wolverine is typical of Lapland. Bear and wolf populations seem to fluctuate, perhaps because of census problems.

There are three species of snake. The viper, which is quite common, is the only poisonous one. Lake Saimaa has its own distinctive species, the ringed seal, which is endangered.

There are 40 species of fish in lakes and in the Baltic, which are adapted to brackish water.

6.1. WHEN IS BEST FOR BIRDWATCHING?

Most Finnish birds are migratory, and make a wonderful view on the south coast as they arrive in spring and leave in autumn. Birds of prey like the sparrow hawk and buzzard turn up in April, and bigger birds like the crane and swan come at the start of May. Geese arrive in great flocks at the end of May, ten thousand or more crossing the sky every hour. Helsinki is often on their path as they head for the arctic.

The reed-filled bays east of Helsinki are ideal for bird spotting during the nesting season: there is a network of towers and hides so birds can be observed without disturbing them. At the close of summer arctic sandpipers are the first to head south, followed by the insect-eaters in August. By late October, the geese, eagles and swans have found their way back to the south of Finland. As the autumn ends, the skies fall quiet again.

6.2. WHAT BERRIES AND MUSHROOMS CAN YOU PICK AND EAT?

The two main forest fruits, whortleberries,

(sometimes called blueberries or bilberries) and lingonberries ("mountain cranberries") are available in great quantities most summers. Arctic bramble rubus arcticus grows only in a narrow belt from North Karelia to Ostrobothnia. Sea buckthorn hippophae rhamnoides grows along the coast. Cloudberries rubus chamaemorus, used to make a distinctive liqueur, prefer the north.

You can pick wild berries and mushrooms almost freely, with the exception of cloudberries in parts of Lapland. The range of wild edible fungi is vast but so is the number of highly inedible types. There are several illustrated Finnish books on wild mushrooms, which indicate graphically which are to be eaten and which avoided. Damp autumn days are the best gathering time.

6.3. HOW MANY THREATENED SPECIES ARE THERE?

Not a lot by international comparison, though information on what is at risk is not always reliable. Mammals have been studied the most. The OECD's Environmental Data report in 1991 concluded that Finland had the second smallest proportion of threatened mammals in Europe, after Norway.

Finnish studies have concluded that there are about 1700 endangered species.

Forestry was the primary cause in nearly half the cases and a contributing factor for many of the rest. The main reason is not the felling of trees as such, but that wetlands have been drained to grow forests, reducing one habitat. Also, cultivated forests are typically young, and dead wood is removed. This takes away another habitat.

6.4. ARE THE BEARS IN THE FOREST DANGEROUS?

Yes, if you sneak up on one without it noticing, but that's hard to do. Most people make a terrible noise (to a bear's ears) and smell (to a bear's nose) as they walk through the woods, and the bear is long gone when they arrive. The greatest risk is if you are walking into a strong wind.

There are hundreds of bears in eastern Finland, though figures are imprecise because they wander back and forth across the Russian border without registering. Every few years some poor soul has a fatal encounter with one but, judging from statistics, fishing is far more dangerous.

cities

There are about 450 municipalities, of which about 140 are urban or semi-urban. About 80% of the Finns live in urban areas. The population (5 million) is concentrated in the south of the country. Nearly one in five Finns lives in the Helsinki metropolitan area, which consists of the neighbouring cities of Helsinki (546,000), Espoo (205,000) and Vantaa (174,000).

The other sizeable towns and cities are (in order of size) Tampere, Turku, Oulu, Lahti, Kuopio, Jyväskylä, Pori, Lappeenranta, Vaasa, Kotka and Joensuu.

43% of households live in apartments and 40% in detached houses. The size of the average dwelling is 76 square metres. There are about 1 million residential buildings and an estimated 2 million saunas.

7.1. WHAT ARE THE COSTS OF BUYING AND RENTING?

There are great variations between different parts of the country and even different parts of the Helsinki metropolitan region. When Finns buy houses, one of their first considerations, after location, is how many square meters of floor space there are. Taking the Helsinki region as an example, the average price per square metre for apartments is about 1700 euros, but a small flat in the inner city could cost twice that while a poor building in an unfashionable area could cost half as much. This price level is about the same as it was ten years ago: there was a slump in between.

The rental market is largely deregulated, and rental income is taxed at the same rate as any other capital investment. This means that rental prices (on the private market, not the city-subsidized one) reflect the price of property and the average rate of interest, offset by expectations about the rise in the value of the property. Interest rates are at record lows and property prices are fairly modest, so rents are reasonable for a European capital.

7.2. HOW CAN YOU RUN A MODERN CITY WHEN IT KEEPS SNOWING?

It doesn't snow all winter but there can be long periods of snowfall, in the south and well as the north. In winter 1998-99, for example, Helsinki was exceptionally snowy. The trick is to be prepared. Cars are required to use studded tyres all winter so they won't skid. When necessary, snowploughs stay out day and night clearing the main roads. Airports are kept open in the same way. Delays on the railways are also usually minimal.

In cities all that snow can't just be pushed to the side of the road. It is loaded onto lorries and carried out of town to dumps. Sometimes these great mounds of ice don't finish thawing till the middle of summer.

7.3. WHY APARTMENTS WHEN THERE'S NO MUCH SPACE FOR HOUSES?

There isn't such a lot of empty space in the areas where people want to live. Inner cities are not run down in Finland; they are desirable residential areas. In other words, apartment buildings are regarded as attractive. Maintenance costs are lower, too. Many households own or have access to a summerhouse in the country, so they aren't stuck in the concrete jungle when the weather is good.

On the other hand, some city administrations, including Helsinki, have a political bias in favour of apartment buildings. Surveys indicate that families would prefer to live in their own house if they could afford one in an area where they could easily get to work and get the kids to school. As wealth grows, the number of single family houses is likely to overtake the number of other dwellings.

7.4. AREN'T HEATING BILLS ASTRONOMICAL?

They would be if the Finns lived in the same kinds of houses as the British or French and heated them in the same way. Triple glazing, standard in Finland, is not the only difference. Walls are thicker and much better insulated. Doors fit doorways and curtains don't move when the wind blows outside. The outer doors of detached houses are usually double, with an airlock between. As a result, houses don't need so much heat in winter and stay cooler in summer.

Most city buildings are connected to a district heating grid. This is a network of sub-street pipes bringing hot water produced by electricity generating stations as a by-product. Many nations still throw this away. Finland uses it to provide central heating for houses. All the extra construction involved does push up property prices but not too much when implemented universally.

People

At the end of 1998 the population totalled 5.1 million (2.5m. men and 2.6m. women). Someone born today can expect to live to 73 is it's a boy, nearly 81 if a girl. 214 people are aged 100 or more, 188 of them women.

The biggest age group is the 45-50 year-olds and the second biggest group is 50-54. This means big changes when they reach retirement. At present only 15% of the population are 65 or more. By 2030 26% will be. Births still exceed deaths but not by much. The population will soon go into reverse. Immigration and emigration are low, not much more than 10,000 a year.

Nominally 85.6% of the Finns are Lutherans but few go to church regularly. About 39% of people are married. 44% of families have one child under 18, 38% have two and 14% have three.

8.1. WHERE DID THE PEOPLE OF FINLAND ORIGINATE?

Because the Finns speak a Uralic language, many people assume that they must have originated in the east. Studies of their DNA don't bear this out. Only a quarter of their genetic stock is Siberian. The rest is European. So it seems likely that an original Uralic people was greatly diluted by contact with Indo-European farming communities, but at a rate slow enough that each wave of newcomers learnt Finnish rather than imposing an Indo-European language.

The Samis of Lapland have a distinctly different genetic profile that is quite unlike other European peoples. Their origin is unclear but they apparently lived for a long period in much greater isolation than the Finns.

8.2. HOW COME THE FIRST SETTLERS PICKED SUCH A COLD PLACE?

It wasn't always so cold. Strangely enough, in the period after the Ice Age, the weather was much milder than today. Great forests of oak and beech reached into the north, where there are only spruce and pine today. This was the time of the Stone Age in Europe. Non-farming societies need large territories so even a small rise in population forces some members to emigrate. Formerly frozen Finland was a good, unoccupied place to hunt, fish and live.

The bronze age with its farming societies nearly passed Finland by because, when Europe reached this stage of development, Finland was no longer very suited for farming. It would have been better earlier.

8.3. DO FINNS HAVE ANY DISTINCT RACIAL OR ETHNIC FEATURES?

The old stereotypes of the shy but honest Finn, moody but efficient, are still much loved by travel writers but don't bear much relation to the younger generation. Their parents were reserved and taciturn because they didn't speak the language of strangers. The young ones talk non-stop. And although you'll still see blondes with high cheekbones with narrow gray eyes, there are others with dark hair, big noses and thick lips.

Honesty and efficiency are cultural characteristics and largely depend on how well a society functions. Finland seem to foster them. The same goes for a penchant for education, an excitement with technology and a love of gadgets.

8.4. ARE THERE MANY FOREIGNERS IN FINLAND?

Not many - 85,000 - but there have been some large changes in the past decade. The most audible is the arrival of Russian speakers. Russian nationals are now the biggest group of foreigners, 17,000 of them. There are also 10,000 Estonians though they don't stand out because Finnish is an easy language for them. Neither group existed before the Soviet Union broke up, ten years ago.

The other very visible group of newcomers is from Somalia, most of whom arrived in 1995. However, there are still only about five thousand. Finland has been very wary of taking large numbers of refugees, partly forewarned by Sweden's experience. There are smaller groups of foreigners from Yugoslavia, Iraq and Vietnam. Of westerners, the three largest national groups are Germans, Britons and US citizens, about two thousand each. (None of the foregoing figures contain foreigners who have taken Finnish nationality.)

Language

Finland has two official languages, Finnish and Swedish, In 1998 there were 92.6 % native Finnish speakers, 5.7 native Swedish speakers and 0.03 % native Lappish speakers.

Most Swedish-speaking Finns mainly live along the coast in the archipelago and in Ostrobothnia on the Gulf of Bothnia. This is a historical phenomenon rather than a racial one. During the long period when Finland and Sweden were one country, many Finnish families switched to Swedish.

Finnish is an odd language for Europe because it is not Indo-European and therefore quite unrelated to Swedish, Russian, English, German or French. It is closely related to Estonian and very distantly to Hungarian. These are members of the Finno-Ugrian group of languages, which are spoken by only about 20 million people in the world.

There are many loan words from Swedish and English but they too are rendered according to Finnish rules of grammar.

9.1. I'VE LEARNT SOME FINNISH AND PEOPLE SAY I SPEAK IT WELL. AM I A GENIUS?

Probably not. Finns have little experience of others speaking their language and are amazed when a foreigner can string half a sentence together. They call this good Finnish.

For the same reason they are unaccustomed to foreign accents, so if you study Finnish for years, you will eventually reach a fluency that they will describe as bad Finnish.

9.2. WHAT ARE SOME USEFUL THINGS TO BE ABLE TO SAY?

The key thing about Finnish is that it is phonetic. Also the stress is always on the first syllable of the word. Once you have mastered pronunciation it is easy to use a phrase books. The tricky vowels for foreigners are "ö", which is somewhere between "a" and "e", and "ö", which is something like an English "er" but pronounced at the front of the mouth. Double vowels are pronounced at twice the length of a single vowel, and double consonants are also doubly pronounced.

Armed with this knowledge you will now have no trouble in saying *kiitos* (thank you), *anteeksi* (sorry) and *saanko* (please can I have). Tea is *tee*, coffee is *kahvi* and beer is *olut*. The numbers one to five are *yksi*, *kaksi*, *kolme*, *neljä* and *viisi*.

9.3. IS THERE ANY POINT LEARNING TO SPEAK FINNISH?

If you can speak English, you can get by nearly everywhere in Finland. German is much less well spoken and French and Russian hardly at all. Swedish is the official second language but, because it is compulsory in school, most young Finns make a point of not learning it. Films on television and in cinemas are subtitled, not dubbed, so foreigners can find entertainment in their own language. The Finnish Broadcasting Company produces news bulletins in English, French, German, Russian and Latin on 103.7 MHz.

But non-Finnish speakers do become isolated, unable to read a daily newspaper, chat casually with strangers, or know what is being said about them. Finnish is also a wonderful secret language for use on trips abroad, enabling you to comment with impunity about the host's food, the policeman's intellect or the waitress' legs.

10.1. WHAT IS IT LIKE TO GROW UP IN FINLAND?

Safe, quiet and, from an outside perspective, dull, but children don't have an outside perspective and are all the better for it. It is a non-hostile environment. Children can go unaccompanied to and from school and play safely in the parks and forests. Firearm incidents usually involve adult drinking partners, not children.

Finnish children are well informed about other countries, particularly in Europe. Increased wealth has allowed most children to travel abroad several times, so it's not ignorance that spares them the perils of others societies. But money does buy trouble, and there are signs of a sharp rise in drug use.

10.2. DAY-CARE MAY BE NICE FOR PARENTS, BUT WHAT ABOUT THE CHILDREN?

The fact that even parents not at work are entitled to day-care places for their children seems like foolish politics. But perhaps it should be seen as part of children's rights, because all the signs are that they like day-care. It's a more stimulating environment than many homes, and teaches them social skills at an early age.

Given that formal schooling begins strangely late in Finland, day-care is a vital part of the learning system and, as funds become available, could certainly be made more effective and educational.

10.3. HOW DOES HIGHER EDUCATION STACK UP AGAINST OTHER EUROPEAN COUNTRIES?

The Finnish university network is one of the densest in Europe. With just 5 million people, there are 20 universities. Ten of them are traditional multi-faculty types, three specialize in engineering and architecture and three teach economics and business. The rest are art academies. 18,000 new students start their studies each year.

Recently the focus has been shifted to natural sciences, medicine and technology and away from the arts and social sciences. Business appreciates this. There are also close links between industry and the polytechnics and other institutions of the university level. It cannot be said that Finnish universities educate their students for unemployment.

11.1. HOW COME WOMEN'S RIGHTS TOOK ROOT SO EARLY IN FINLAND?

Because it was such a poor, agricultural country. When the growing season is short, work has to be done quickly. Men and women traditionally worked alongside each other on the land. When industrialization got under way, it didn't strike them as strange to work together in factories. Leisured "upper class" values never took root because the number of wealthy people was so small.

The Second World War probably helped to cement the idea of women in important work. The whole nation was mobilized to resist the Red Army's attack and, while the men did the fighting, the women took over all the jobs left behind. After the war ended they didn't go home.

11.2. HOW DOES WOMEN'S PAY COMPARE WITH MEN'S?

A century of complete political equality has not translated into equal pay. Women's salaries in both the private and the public sector are still only about 75% of men's salaries. This is partly because there is a clear division between the jobs that men and women set their sights on. For example, teaching, health care and social work are female domains.

Things could go either way in future. More flexible employment contracts might weaken the position of women on the labour market. On the other hand, the growing need for continuous education of employees would seem to favour the sex that shows more academic ability.

11.3. WHAT'S THE POLITICAL FUSS ABOUT UNEMPLOYMENT BENEFITS?

It's true that they are only 13% of all welfare spending, which is far less than, for example, care of the elderly. But unemployment benefit is part of the structural problem of Finnish public finances. Finland has recent experience of this, because a serious slump in the early 1990s pushed unemployment to record levels.

The government raises a large part of its budget by taxing wages, so when unemployment is high, and you have the greatest need for revenue to pay for benefits, taxes yield the least, and the result is a large deficit. This does not mean that the unemployed should not receive welfare payments, though how much they get does affect incentive.

Disease, Crime

The leading causes of death in 1996 were cardiovascular, respiratory and gastrointestinal diseases, and tumours. Nearly 10% of deaths are caused by acts of violence or accidents. About a quarter of these acts are suicides.

There are about 150 acts of murder or manslaughter each year. This is a rather high homicide rate by European standards but the rate for assaults is about the same as Sweden's. Nearly half of serious offences are theft or robbery.

Cases of drunken driving are stable at about 20 thousand a year. There are less than half as many offences involving narcotics but the number is on the rise.

12.1. WHY DO MANY FINNISH PEOPLE KILL THEMSELVES?

For a long time Finland took second place in the suicide table after Hungary. Although there is a linguistic relationship between Finnish and Hungarian, it is tenuous and not matched on the genetic or pathological level. And today the Baltic States, Russia, Belarus, Sri Lanka and Slovenia also have more suicides per head than Finland. So the reasons for killing oneself are obviously many and complex.

On a world scale, Finns still have a high propensity for suicide, especially young males. Nearly half of Finnish adult suicides are by people with an alcohol problem but this is not true of the young. Studies have also turned up the paradox that suicide in Finland becomes more common at a time of faster economic growth. The last slump, despite all the bankruptcies and dismissals, cut the suicide rate. There are no good general theories.

12.2. WHY IS THERE SO MUCH HEART DISEASE?

Cardio-vascular disease has yielded to scientific analysis and action quite well. There is a genetic disposition towards it, which has been amplified by diet and lifestyle. The theory was proven in the North Karelia project, launched in 1972 in response to exceptionally high heart disease rates in that area of Finland.

The project aimed at health through educating the public and it worked. By 1995 deaths from heart disease were down 75%. Lung cancer also fell. But the Finns are still the most overweight people in the Nordic area, which is reflected not only in blood cholesterol but also in a tendency to diabetes.

12.3. WHY IS FINLAND SOFT ON CRIME?

It seems so if you look at the Finnish jail system. There's no death penalty, of course, and the number of prisoners is at one of the lowest levels in Europe. There are only about 50 people serving life, and in practice a life sentence usually means 10-15 years. A lot of prisoners spend time studying. If only a few dozen bother to escape, surely something is wrong?

Or you can look at it another way: that prisons are the universities of crime, where unstable or antisocial beginners are separated from the civilized world and given an expert education in how to turn their unhappy tendencies into a lifelong career.

13.1. HOW DID THE ECONOMY COPE WITH POST-WAR REPARATIONS?

The cost of goods and supplies forfeited to the Soviet Union was staggering, an estimated 570 million dollars at 1952 prices, which was roughly 80% of GDP. This obligation was imposed on a country that was already exhausted from war. Some Finns believed the schedule was impossible but winning the peace with gifts was less onerous than losing the war with blood. The shipments lasted about seven years.

The irony was that the Soviet Union, which though it was getting a free lunch, got hooked. When the reparations stopped, the Russians started buying the same goods. A new export sector had been created.

13.2. WHAT HAS MADE A COUNTRY WITHOUT RESOURCES WEALTHY?

It's true that Finland lacks fossil fuels (not counting peat). It has a fair amount of hydroelectric capacity, but this is been fully harnessed already. It is not self-sufficient in any metal ores, although there are sizeable copper and nickel deposits. The only major resource is the forest, which was long the source of most exports.

Steady economic growth seems to depend little on natural resources. It hinges on human capital, using highly trained people to create goods and processes more efficiently than before. The Japanese, renowned for their large numbers but negligible mineral resources, showed the way. Now Finland is showing that it can be done with a small population.

13.3. WAS IT THE SOVIET COLLAPSE THAT CAUSED THE 1990S SLUMP?

At one time during the 1980s the Soviet Union was buying a quarter of Finnish exports - ice breakers, complete factories, even cities. Exports to Russia plunged after 1991. The idea that this caused the great Finnish slump of the early 1990s is attractive, doubly so because it absolves Finnish leaders still in positions of power. But Finland's economic disaster and banking crisis were homemade.

The roots of the slump lay in the 1980s, when industrial costs got out of control. Falling price competitiveness was what had made Finland dependent on easy (and corrupt) Soviet trade.

Exports fell from a 35% of GDP to 20%. Industry piled up new debts with inefficient investments. Management was equally feeble in banking. Without the loss of the Russian market the crisis would probably have happened anyway, slightly later.

13.4. WHY WERE THE FINNS READY TO GIVE UP THEIR "MARKKA"?

European Monetary Union supposedly sent shivers down German spines, shocked at the prospect of swapping the mark that had brought so much stability and wealth for the untried euro. Yet Finnish leaders set their sights on EMU even when it looked as if they would not be eligible. There was little sentimentality about the Finnish markka.

Because it has not been so stable. The Finns persuaded Czar Alexander to let them have their own currency in 1865 by telling him that the rouble was too big for their little economy. In fact they just wanted to escape the vast, uncertain rouble zone. Obviously the markka has been a better store of value than the rouble but the euro is going to be in a class apart.

Law

Finland has strong constitutional protection of private property. This extends to pension rights and limits the extent to which the law can encroach on labour market agreements.

There is freedom of occupation, although obviously some activities are licensed. The favourite form of business incorporation is the limited company. There are no separate courts for civil and penal matters. There are general courts of justice, plus six courts of appeal in different parts of the country. The Supreme Court is the highest instance. It normally sits with five members. Precedents are not legally binding except, in practice, on the Supreme Court.

14.1. ISN'T IT DANGEROUS NOT TO HAVE JURIES?

This rests on the assumption that judges might be even more capricious that juries. Finland does not have a jury system but the panel of judges in local court does have a large lay element. Only the chairman of the court must be learned in law. The other three or four judges are not lawyers, and their votes have as much weight as the learned judge.

Supreme Court judges tend to have a background as judges, but some have been university professors, Justice Ministry officials or attorneys at law. Perhaps the key difference in Finnish courts is that judges are more likely to believe in the effectiveness and benevolence of the legal (and police) system than juries might.

14.2. IS THERE ONE LAW FOR THE RICH AND ANOTHER FOR THE POOR?

In any legal system, the rich man can buy more expensive counsel. But some critics say that a system without juries has an extra weakness because it is so detached from normal, everyday life. Judges are naturally far closer to business and political decisionmakers than the man in the street, let alone the criminal in the street. This is reflected in a more indulgent attitude towards "better folk" who go astray.

Recently, a Supreme Court judge, whose family had been implicated in tax evasion, put forward the principle that, if a wealthy man and a poor man steal the same amount, the former's guilt is less because the sum is less important to him. A scandal erupted and denials were issued but a sense of public unease remained.

14.3. WHY AREN'T CONTRACTS STRICTLY ENFORCED?

For the first half of the 20th century, Finnish courts stuck very closely to the written word of contracts and demanded strict fulfillment of contractual obligations. The three principles of contract law were then freedom, reliance and balance. Since the Second World War, a fourth principle has been added and constantly boosted: protection of the weaker party.

A good example is the statutory guarantee; the buyer cannot sign away his rights. Consumer protection boards and agencies are an extension of the same. Finland is far from unique in this but has taken the principle farther than many countries. Indeed, some Finns think that "the State as nanny" has gone too far.

14.4. WHY DO THE COURTS AWARD SUCH LOW DAMAGES?

Because the damages are set by judges, not by juries. Also because of the principle that, in a welfare state, the community is responsible for providing basic security to everyone. This is particularly clear in the case of personal injuries. The tariff for lost limbs and other body parts is ungenerous.

There are other principles involved that are sometimes ignored by juries elsewhere. One is that minor breaches of norms should not entail heavy compensation for remote consequences, such as if a wrongly parked car stops the fire brigade getting close enough to stop a building burning down. Every act has countless untold consequences. The worst ones can be equally accidental.

Conſtitution

Finland is an independent republic. The president is elected to a six-year term, and can serve only two consecutive terms. A 200-member, single-chamber parliament is elected every four years. The prime minister of a government with a strong majority has far more power than the President.

Members of parliament are chosen by proportional representation. As a result, no party ever achieves close to an absolute majority, and governments are formed by coalition. The prime minister is appointed by parliament, not by the president.

15.1. WHERE HAS THE PRESIDENT'S POWER GONE?

Until fairly recently, Finland resembled France in concentrating great power in the President's hands; to determine foreign policy and to make and break governments. These prerogatives were used ruthlessly by the first post-war president, Urho Kekkonen, but his successor, Mauno Koivisto, moved Finland in the direction of parliamentarianism. At the same time, parliament and governments became more stable.

Koivisto's successor, Martti Ahtisaari, was a figurehead in domestic politics. A constitutional reform in 1999 also trimmed the president's role in making foreign policy.

15.2. HOW DOES PROPORTIONAL REPRESENTATION WORK?

Finland is divided into 15 electoral districts. The number of members of parliament from each district depends on its population. A party fields a list of candidates for a certain district. Each voter has one vote. The outcome is calculated by electoral district, using the d'Hondt method.

First the number of votes received by each candidate is counted. Then personal votes are added together by party list. The candidate on the list receiving the largest number of personal votes is deemed to have received all the votes cast for people on that list. The candidate with the second highest vote gets half of the votes cast for the list, the third one third, and so on. Then these notional votes are combined into one table and the top candidates are elected. If the district can send, say, ten members to parliament, the jobs go to the top ten.

15.3. WOULDN'T A SIMPLER SYSTEM PRODUCE A CLEARER OUTCOME?

This proportional representation system ensures that the number of MPs from each party in parliament is about the same as the distribution of votes between parties. It's a bit unfair to small parties, though they can try to redress it by forming electoral alliances.

The odd results come when one candidate is so enormously popular that his or her total vote is enough to elect other candidates from the same list, even if hardly anyone voted for them. That's the price you pay for a system that produces fewer "wasted" votes.

15.4. WHO DECIDES WHAT LAWS ARE CONSTITUTIONAL?

The Supreme Court is for appeals only; no court has the authority to strike down laws deemed unconstitutional. And although the constitution requires parliament to handle certain types of legislation using special procedures, parliament (in its Constitutional Committee) itself decides what this applies to. It sounds like putting the fox in charge of the henhouse, and it has been abused in the past.

The latest constitutional reform, taking effect in March 2000, requires the courts to give precedence to the Constitution in cases where the strict application of a law would be in conflict with the constitution. So although no court can rule on a law in general, it could refuse to apply it.

Government

Governments in Finland are almost always coalitions, at least if they want to enjoy a majority in parliament which, now that the president has few powers, has become vital. With the three largest parties roughly equal in size, a variety of coalitions is usually viable. It's a matter for negotiation. Inter-party talks also determine which ministries are formed and who gets which.

Local government is also very important, though it attracts less glory. There are 452 local authorities, consisting of municipalities and cities. Finland is divided into six provinces but these have little practical significance.

16.1. WHICH ARE THE KEY MINISTRIES IN THE GOVERNMENT?

The power lies where the money is. The foremost in recent years has been the Finance Ministry, which oversees taxation and expenditure. Then comes Industry, responsible for economic policies and still quite a lot of state-owned enterprise. With the growing role of infrastructure, Communications is rising in stature.

Although fairly important, the Ministry for Foreign Affairs overlaps with the domains of the prime minister and the president. So does Defence. The European Union overshadows Agriculture & Forestry. The single most thankless ministry is Labour and will remain so, now that fiscal prudence prevents the creation of false jobs.

16.2. WHY ARE THERE SO MANY GOVERNMENT MINISTERS?

There are 13 ministries and an even larger number of ministers - 17 - not including the prime minister. The Ministry of Labour would be abolished if this could be done without sending the wrong message to the still-numerous unemployed. At least it could be combined with Education. Two more pairs of ministries could also be usefully combined.

But a coalition government needs more ministerial seats, not fewer. The tiny parties in the coalition need to show that they are doing a big job, but can't be allowed a number of seats in the cabinet that is very disproportionate to the big parties. This is why there are two ministers at Finance, Industry, the Interior and Social Affairs. One is usually very much the junior.

16.3. WHY ARE GOVERNMENT TERMS GETTING LONGER?

Finnish coalitions used to be fragile, rather short-lived affairs, often collapsing suddenly amid policy disputes or when the president signified his displeasure. This has been changing. In 1987 the government set a record by surviving for the full four years of the parliamentary term. Now that the next three governments have done the same, it has become the norm.

This is partly a response to necessity. Because the president is now a figurehead, a government collapse would leave a serious power vacuum. Conversely, it is greater political maturity that has allowed the president's powers to be trimmed. In particular, parties negotiating for government position are now better at foreseeing contentious issues and working out a compromise in advance.

16.4. WHAT MATTERS ARE HANDLED AT THE MUNICIPAL LEVEL?

Public services like education, social welfare and health care, maintaining technical infrastructure, and also some taxation. Sometimes municipalities co-operate, for example in running hospitals. Sometimes they are in competition, such as in setting the local income tax rate. There is no upper tax limit, but any area that pitches its rate too high will gradually lose residents to neighbouring areas, so the acceptable level of expenditure needs to be carefully thought through. In 1998 the lowest local rate was 15% and the highest 19.75%. (This is on top of national income tax).

About half of spending comes from local tax. Subsidies from the central government provide another 13% and most of the rest is raised by various charges.

Politics

There are three major parties, the Social Democrats, the Centre Party, and the Conservatives (who use the name Coalition Party). The demise of the fourth major player, the Communist Party (which also called itself something else) has simplified the government question. The one that wins the biggest vote in elections picks which of the other two it wants to govern with.

After the 1999 general election the parties in parliament were the Social Democratic Party (22.9% of votes), the Centre Party (22.4%), the National Coalition Party (21.0%), the Left Wing Alliance (10.9%), the Green League (7.3%), the Swedish People's Party (5.1%), the Finnish Christian Union (4.2%) the Reform Group (1.1%) and the True Finns 1.1%.

17.1. WHAT DO THE SOCIAL
DEMOCRATS STAND FOR?

Traditionally backed by urban workers, the Social Democratic Party believes in egalitarian income distribution but not to the extent of killing the golden goose by taxing business and industry heavily. In government it has overseen slow and pragmatic privatization.

The party has long-standing ties with the main industrial labour unions and believes in a tripartite approach (unions, employers, and government) to holding down costs and inflation and keeping up the growth rate. So far it has worked, at the cost of structural inflexibility.

17.2. WHERE DOES THE
CENTRE STAND FOR?

Originally drawing its support from the countryside, the party tried to follow its supporters into the cities as Finland became urbanized. Its success ensured it a continuing place among the big three parties but split it into opposing rural and urban factions, particularly over the EU.

In government the party's leaders courageously

led Finland into the EU, but have been dragging their feet in opposition ever since. Centrist attempts to open up a debate in other areas, such the labour market and job flexibility, have so far been fiercely rebuffed by Social Democratic interest groups. The Centre's own umbilical interest group, the Farmers' Union, has fallen on hard times.

17.3. HOW CONSERVATIVE ARE THE CONSERVATIVES?

The National Coalition Party shifted towards the centre in the 1970s, as it became clear that traditional conservatism would be a permanent barrier to entering a Finnish government during the Cold War era. Although this tactic didn't get it into government till 1987, it did help pick up new middle class votes.

This is the party of upwardly mobile employees and professionals, rather than the poodle of big business. Like the Centre, it tries to embrace town and country alike, but because it is less conservative than the Centre Party in many ways, it finds the experience less divisive.

17.4. WHAT ABOUT THE FAR LEFT AND GREENS?

The old Communist Party went bankrupt in the early 1990s, following property speculation. This ignominious fate made it easier to purge the new Left-Wing Alliance and position it as a modern, dogma-free party that cares. A member of two governments since then, the Far Left has proved that it has no quarrel with liberal market economics.

The Green League has been the only successful smaller party in recent years. It joined the government coalition in 1995, a world first. It stuck in there for the full government term, showing that impatience with whatever harms the environment can be accommodated within political compromise. Like the Far Left, the Greens have moved from speak-ill to feel-good.

Political history

After the Winter and Continuation Wars, Finland avoided occupation by the Soviet Union but was saddled with a Treaty on Friendship, Co-operation and Mutual Assistance.

A key aim of post-war foreign policy was to keep good and stable relations with Moscow without falling into its camp. The parallel aim was to develop ties with democratic western Europe without antagonizing Russia.

In the late 1950s Moscow's suspicions blocked the creation of a Nordic economic zone, but in 1955 Finland joined the UN and the Nordic Council.

By 1961, Finland took associate membership status of EFTA, and in 1973 signed a free trade agreement with the European Community.

18.1. WHAT DID FINLANDIZATION MEAN?

Finlandization was coined in the 1970s to mean deferring to another, more powerful country without any force being applied. It was often used in the sense of a process, where politicians, the press and eventually the public learn to suppress critical instincts. The word was popular among right-wing political scientists, and very unpopular among Finnish leaders.

Up to the 1980s the Finns did perceive a strong threat from the Soviet Union. Any Finnish journalist or politician who worked at the time knows that there was self-censorship on issues that would have upset Moscow. One taboo subject was the feeling of threat. Another was the Soviet occupation of Karelia, which many Finns would have liked to recover. There were other such subjects.

Publicity was never a good way of putting pressure on Moscow. In the Karelian question, behind-the-scenes pressure didn't work either. But in tactful silence, Finnish leaders retained a western democracy, stymied post-war Communist attempts at a coup and resisted all Soviet calls for military cooperation.

18.2. WHY DIDN'T FINLAND TAKE A TOUGHER LINE TOWARDS MOSCOW?

In the early post-war period it wouldn't have been a good

idea. The Soviet Union was one of the winners of the Second World War and Finland one of the losers, although Finland's war had been against the Soviet Union, not against Britain or America. Until the late 1970s Moscow still saw Finland as part of its sphere of interest and although the western powers supported Finland politically and economically, it is very unlikely anyone would have come to its military defence.

By the 1980s the Finns could have been ruder but that would have done nothing more than damage trade. By then the Soviet Union was, for Finland, an unthreatening neighbour.

18.3. WAS ECONOMIC INTEGRATION WITH THE EAST AN OPTION?

This concept was invented to ease Finnish economic moves in a westerly direction, though some naive politicians took it seriously. When the free-trade agreement was signed with EFTA in 1961, another was signed with the Soviet Union, freeing Soviet imports from Finnish customs duties at the same rate as EFTA's. When the free-trade agreement was signed with the European Community in 1963, a parallel agreement was signed with the East European trading bloc, the CMEA.

A lot more eastern trade would not have been good for Finland because eastern economies were not designed around the principle of comparative advantage, where one concentrates on what one does best. CMEA production was assigned on political or often quite random grounds. This leads to shoddy products that don't keep competitors up to scratch. The only success story in eastern trade was Finland-Russia because the Russians had a product that couldn't go wrong: oil.

18.4. WHY HAS FINLAND BEEN SO ACTIVE AT THE UN?

Finns have a strong belief in human rights and the peaceful settlement of disputes. But during the Cold War, organizations like the Council of Europe were treated by socialist countries as a western conspiracy of interference. This left only the United Nations where Finland could advance its principles without appearing to take sides.

Finns have not only been busy UN bureaucrats but also active UN peacekeepers all over the world. This has been very popular with the Finnish public; just as well because they have had to foot the bill. A temporary job in a world hot spot has also meant a welcome change for Finnish servicemen, with the bonus of being able to bring home a car duty-free at the end of it. (Total sales tax on automobiles in Finland is about 140%.)

EU

Finland is one of the newest members of the European Union, having joined in 1995 at the same time as Sweden and Austria. This followed a decisive referendum result in Finland and a rather narrower one in Sweden. Norwegians rejected membership.

Although the honeymoon is over, the EU remains more popular among Finns than Swedes. One reason is that Finland feels EU membership contributes to national security.

Finland strongly supports EU enlargement, particularly involving the Baltic States, and would like to see greater cooperation between the EU and Russia. It also believes in more EU foreign policy co-ordination.

19.1. WHY DIDN'T FINLAND JOIN THE EU EARLIER?

Because of business and foreign politics. While its important trading partners, Britain and Sweden, remained outside the EU (then the European Community), Finland was better off as a member of EFTA. Also the Soviet Union, not the easiest of neighbours in the Cold War, was very wary of the political aspirations of Brussels and exerted great influence over Finnish policies.

By the 1990s, when EFTA had become a distinctly second-class club, it looked briefly as if the only way of combining good business with political expediency was the European Economic Area, a merger between EFTA and the European Community on a merely economic level. Fortunately the Soviet Union then fell apart so the dilemma disappeared and Finland could move straight on to EU membership.

19.2. HOW DO FINNISH FARMERS FEEL ABOUT IT?

Most farmers were against the EU because they had enjoyed a system of price subsidies so generous that even the EU's exorbitant Common Agricultural

Policy looked stingy by comparison. EU accession brought cuts in producer prices of 50% or even more. Egg prices fell more than 75%.

Farmers now receive much of their subsidies as direct cash payments based on cultivated hectares or the number of animals. Other sources of complaint are the inspections and paperwork. But EU shock treatment has had a beneficial effect on farming, focussing attention on matters like quality, demand and marketing, which were irrelevant under the old system of subsidies.

19.3. WHAT HAS CHANGED MOST AND LEAST?

Food prices dropped sharply during the first year of EU membership and have largely stayed down. This has meant a solid increase in the purchasing power of consumers. Another big change has been in competition policy, which previously banned cartels but not outright mergers that would restrict competition. This too has probably helped hold prices down.

The end of duty-free sales in the EU will not affect Baltic shipping much because traffic between Finland and Sweden can be re-routed to pass via Estonia or the Åland Islands. National gambling and alcohol distribution monopolies still exist, though this may still change. High local rates of tax on alcohol and cars will have to be reduced one day soon but the government will keep them high as long as possible because they yield so much revenue.

19.4. WHAT DOES THE "NORTHERN DIMENSION" MEAN?

It means a harmonization of policies towards the northern regions near to the EU. It is not a new programme, and could even mean savings. Put bluntly, the EU has been pumping money into Russia (among others) without achieving much for itself or for Russia. It needs a co-ordinated policy with specific objectives and, often, a business-oriented approach to achieving them.

Finland would like to see the construction of a gas pipeline linking Siberian (and future Barents) gas fields with central Europe via the Baltic area, a route that is shorter than the current line through central Europe. This would link Nordic consumers to the European gas market. Efforts to improve nuclear safety in Northeast Europe and reduce air and waterborne pollution might also benefit from being brought under the Northern Dimension umbrella.

Defence

The national policy is total defence of Finnish territory using a large reserve army, founded on general conscription. This means that Finland could mobilize more than half a million trained soldiers if necessary.

In peacetime the armed forces total about 35,000 funded with an annual budget of 1.5 billion euros. Finland remains outside all military alliances although it signed a Partnership for Peace document with NATO in 1994.

There are hopes for closer cooperation with neutral Sweden and NATO-member Norway in purchases of equipment, particularly the combat helicopters that the army wants for its rapid deployment force.

20.1. WHAT ARE THE MILITARY LESSONS OF HISTORY?

Finland's most enduring memory of the Winter War was its isolation but there were other lessons, too. Military capacity needs to be visible and credible - Stalin attacked because he thought he could take over in a few weeks. The Finnish army was under-equipped, but its will and skill were enough to offset superior Soviet firepower. Also the Finns learnt that a small state does not need to defeat a larger opponent, just to hold it off long enough to make a diplomatic settlement attractive.

The first post-war change was the development of nuclear technology but this failed to render conventional forces unnecessary. More recently the collapse of the Soviet Union lifted political and military pressure, though introducing new elements of uncertainty. Today Finland is no longer so small: the official GDP of Russia, for example, is only three times larger. Also, developments in transport and technology have reduced Finland's isolation.

20.2. WHY DOES FINLAND STILL HAVE CONSCRIPTION?

Because it's cheap, it works and Dad did it. All Finnish men are liable for military service between the ages of 17 and 60. They are called up when 18, unless they volunteer when 17 or obtain a postponement because of studies or other special reasons. Depending on the training they choose/receive, service lasts six month, nine months or a year.

General Staff likes to point out that Belgium's professional army costs nearly 50% more than Finland's, to defend a tiny country under no discernible threat. Finland simply couldn't afford a professional army strong enough to defend its great territory, they say. This is sophistry. An army of conscripts comes cheap only when you do not pay them normal wages. But Finns, it seems, would prefer this to paying even more taxes. And what else would men talk about when they get old?

20.3. WHAT ABOUT WOMEN AND CONSCIENTIOUS OBJECTORS?

Young women aren't called up, as young men are. The top brass is worried about the effect of seething hormones on training: most people are called up for active duty in their late teens. Women can now volunteer but not many do, which may be an indication of how popular female conscription would be.

A conscript with reasons of conscience or religion for refusing to carry arms can opt for non-combatant service of 11 months. Someone who cannot bear to be associated with the armed forces can do civilian social service of 13 months. Some complain that the extra time - one month more than the maximum for ordinary conscripts - is a form of punishment, but perhaps some premium is needed to make a fairly useless activity unattractive.

20.4. WHEN WILL FINLAND JOIN NATO?

The official line is that membership of NATO is unnecessary because Finland has no security problems that it would solve. Therefore a debate is unnecessary. Some remember that the same used to be said about EU membership. The unspoken element is the attitude of Russia, which came to accept the EU but still reacts with instinctive hostility to the name of its old military adversary. NATO expansion in the Baltic region could mean less security for Finland, rather than more.

A 1995 Finnish government report noted that security problems go beyond military issues to include political instability, regional and internal conflicts, uncontrolled movements of population and ethnic disputes. Given the inactivity of other international organizations, Finland had sympathy with NATO actions against the Serbian evacuation of Kosovo. But the ideal Finnish scenario would be the creation of a coherent EU foreign policy, backed up by force and able to call for assistance from across the Atlantic. NATO by another name.

Public finances

Government taxation and spending patterns were seriously shaken by the great recession that hit the Finnish economy in the early 1990s. Public spending controls were introduced and some items of spending were cut, but soaring welfare expenditure at a time of falling tax revenue led to sizeable budget deficits. In 1990, total central government debt was about 10% of GDP. Six years later it was nearly 67%.

Since then the tide has turned because fast economic growth has boosted GDP and tax revenue. At the same time, expenditure has been brought under control by setting spending limits on the main ministries for several years ahead. The budget now shows a small surplus.

21.1. WHY ARE TAXES SO HIGH?
DO FINNS LIKE THEM?

Though you will win no Finnish friends by suggesting so, it is the only explanation. Taxes take a massive 48% of GDP (1996 figures) compared with 38% in Germany. The Finns have endless patience with changes in tax rates, complex deductibility rules and bizarre new taxes. Candidates for parliament frequently campaign on a platform of the new complications they want to build into the tax system. And get elected.

In recent years Finland has endured steadily rising rates of capital tax, constantly changing income tax allowances and special taxes on package holidays and telephone calls, to mention a few. The old silly idea to be struck down was the environment minister's call for a levy of 10,000 markkas on new summerhouses.

21.2. HOW DID FINLAND MEET
THE EMU CRITERIA?

The rules for participation in the third stage of Economic and Monetary Union - adoption of the euro - were laid down in the Maastricht Treaty, signed in 1992. Finland was not a member of the EU at the time. It wouldn't have seemed likely to meet the conditions anyway, because it had a history of high inflation. Total government borrowing was low but rising fast because the budget deficit was widening. And the exchange rate was certainly not stable.

By 1996 Finland, then an EU member, was recovering so fast that the convergence criteria were in reach. The awful slump had killed inflation. The debt ratio was levelling off because spending was being controlled while GDP rose. In the end, even the budget deficit ceiling was achieved because the large surplus on privately run pension funds was counted by Maastricht as part of the public sector.

21.3. ARE CAPITAL TAXES TOO LIGHT?

Comparatively so, yes, but not in absolute terms. Shaken by the slump, parliament enacted a breathtaking reform of capital taxation in 1992. Not only was the tax rate lowered to 25%. Various allowances were also abolished, and the same rate was applied to all capital earnings, from corporate profits to rental income. The tax has been very successful at generating revenue, but politicians have been regretting it ever since.

This is because taxation of wages is far higher, including a top marginal income tax rate of 62%.

The government has agreed to raise the capital tax rate a couple of times but the gap with personal taxation is still wide. The fundamental problem is that personal taxation cannot be lowered because the budget would go into deficit. Higher capital tax would not generate enough revenue to allow a meaningful cut in personal tax. Higher consumption taxes would, but VAT is already 22%.

21.4. WHERE DOES ALL THE MONEY GO?

Cradle-to-grave security does not come cheap, especially at the extremities. The very young and the very old receive far more than they give. According to calculations by the Government Institute for Economic Research, a Finnish 1-year-old has already received benefits from society worth over 15,000 euros in terms of health services, hospital costs and various allowances to the parents.

A schoolchild receives a net 10,000 euros a year from the state. By the age of 24, he or she has accumulated net benefits from the state of 160,000 euros. Only at this age does the citizen start to pay more in taxes than he receives in benefits. And not until the age of 48 has he paid back all the benefits received earlier. Dying young is a shame for everyone.

Trade

The European Union accounts for 60% of Finland's imports and 56% of exports. This is not an exceptionally high proportion and means that Finland is prone to price and market shocks from outside the EU.

16% of exports go to other parts of Europe, 11% to Asia and 8% to North America. The balance of trade moved out of deficit in 1991, when the slump wiped out domestic purchasing power. The surplus then grew steadily as the economy recovered, because growth was export-led.

The current account has been in surplus since 1994.

22.1. WHAT DOES THE EU MEAN FOR TRADE FIGURES?

Since EU accession in 1995, trade between Finland and other members of the Union has no longer been subject to Customs control. National statistics for trade are therefore partly compiled from surveys of companies. Only trade with the rest of the world is still based on customs declarations.

Finland's largest trading partners are in the EU. Germany buys 12% of Finnish exports and provides 15% of imports. Then come Sweden and the UK. Next is the United States. In 1998, Russia was the fifth largest individual market, but its share has certainly been pushed down by the rouble crisis and devaluation. In time, EMU will serve to boost trade between its members because there is no currency risk.

22.2. WHAT DOES FINLAND SELL TO AND BUY FROM THE WORLD?

Of imports 40% are intermediate goods – raw materials, components, etc. This is high figure because Finland has limited natural resources. In many cases the finished product is re-exported. The other categories of import are investment goods (27%), consumer goods (24%) and energy (8%).

The old clichÈ that Finnish exports stand on two legs, one wooden and one metal, is no longer true now that electrical equipment has become the largest single category (26%). Paper products are next (24%). Machinery, equipment and metal products are also important (21%).

22.3. WHY HAVE ELECTRONICS EXPORTS OVERTAKEN EVERYTHING ELSE?

The rise of the electronics sector began long before the boom in mobile communications equipment. It was a natural direction for the engineering industry, which wanted to get into areas of greater value-added than mechanical machinery. Initially the move into bulk electronics was not very profitable: Finland lacked any advantage in manufacturing products like tv sets. This changed with the take-off in communications equipment because the North of Europe was a pioneering area and therefore an ideal test-bed.

In 1998, all other export sectors suffered setbacks. Yet demand for communications equipment was so strong that total exports continued to grow. There's some concern that Finland is becoming too dependent on electronics and electrical equipment, but this misses the main point. Without this diversification, the economy would now be much less healthy.

22.4. WHAT'S THE POINT OF A SURPLUS UNDER EMU?

For years Finland suffered from chronic trade deficits, currency crises and devaluations. Now it has now achieved constant surpluses, just when monetary union means that this makes no difference to the exchange rate and has to be shared with the rest of the euro-area. But it's ironic only when viewed from the old national standpoint. What matters today is the success of enterprises. A big Finnish surplus means that Finnish-based companies are competitive and dynamic. This means more profits and employment, and attracts more investment from abroad.

The old concepts of a virtuous surplus and dishonourable deficit were misleading, anyway. A country running a permanent surplus was depriving itself of what it had earned.

Spending

After the slump of the early 1990s, when many Finnish households suffered a severe fall in living standards, the economy has now bounced back and the people are richer than ever.

The savings rate went above 10% in 1992. Now it is down at 2% and domestic demand is strong.

Households now spend more money on housing than any other category. This is a recent change. Spending on food used to be more. It was high for Europe because Finnish food prices were high. EU membership made food cheaper.

Families are focussing their new wealth on "quality-of-life" goods. For most people that means where they live. Spending on transport and communications remains high, because automobiles and fuel are taxed so heavily.

23.1. WHAT IS THE COST OF LIVING LIKE?

The cost of living depends on how high Finnish prices. For foreign visitors, the cost level varies according to the exchange rate, too, but rates have now been permanently fixed inside the euro area, as a prelude to the switch to euros. So, within the euro area, cost comparisons are now straightforward. Finland's prices are high. Only Sweden and Denmark are more expensive. Compared with all western Europe, the Finnish price level is about 14% above average.

One reason is that the standard rate of tax on goods and services, VAT, is a high 22% in Finland. It is also high in Sweden and Denmark. Another factor is that food is expensive. EU membership lowered food prices but not to the average level. It's thought that European Monetary Union will bring them down some more. In time it will probably also force harmonization of tax rates. But in the meantime, Finland will be relatively expensive.

23.2. DO YOU NEED A LOCAL HELSINKI STOCK EXCHANGE?

It was thought at one time that local stock exchanges would by killed off by giant regional exchanges, just as hypermarkets have replaced so many European corner stores. Indeed, most city stock exchanges have died but national ones have so far survived in Europe, because of differences in language and custom. Also, a local stock exchange represents a fund of more knowledge about local companies than a continental exchange could.

This only works if the local market is fast, efficient and cheap so the Helsinki Stock Exchange merged with the Finnish derivatives exchange and the securities depository to form the HEX Group. Then HEX did a deal with the Frankfurt Exchange and Europe's largest derivatives exchange, Eurex, that will make it into their "branch office" in the North. At the same time HEX shares and financial products become available throughout Europe.

23.3. WHY DON'T ORDINARY FINNS BUY SHARES?

Although it is rising, equity investment by private individuals is still relatively low in Finland. The main reason is the stranglehold that Finnish banks used to have on the financial sector. A tightly knit network of cross-ownership linked the banks, the insurance companies and major private enterprises. Companies borrowed investment capital from their banks, and banks obtained their funding from bank deposits. The stock exchange was a snooty club. The banks controlled it, as well as having the bank inspectorate in their pocket.

This comfortable and grossly wasteful system fell

apart in the banking crisis of the early 1990s, when the banks faced bankruptcy. Several collapsed. Now, as the public gets over the shock of learning that risk exists, money is flowing into an equity market eager to serve. Mutual funds are expanding faster in Finland than anywhere else in Europe. Only pension funds have yet to wake up and are still dreaming of risk-free investment.

23.4. WHERE WILL THE MONEY BE IN FUTURE?

This is the question every entrepreneur asks himself. A key factor is that the average age is increasing and there will soon be more elderly people than ever before or ever again. But it is a mistake to assume that they will all be retired. To maintain economic growth and welfare, many will have to be persuaded to continue working.

This means a boom in demand, not for "Twilight Years" rest homes, but for services that make employment feasible and attractive for the elderly. Health monitoring, dietary programmes and financial counselling are some of the services that will move in the direction of the workplace. Other incentives will be provision of transport and better telecommuting facilities, and this in turn spells some repopulation of rural areas.

Employment

Employment by sector, 1998 %

Services	66
Secondary production	28
Primary production	6

Employer, 1998 %

Private	71
Municipality	22
State	7

Job, 1998 %

Permanent full-time	76
Fixed-term full-time	13
Permanent part-time	7

*1998 unemployment rate 11.4%,
employment rate 64,1%*

24.1. WHY DON'T THE UNEMPLOYMENT RATE AND THE EMPLOYMENT RATE ADD UP?

Finland's real unemployment rate went above 20% of the labour force in the first half of the 1990s. Such a high rate was politically unacceptable. Since jobs could not be created by decree, the answer was to massage the figures by taking people off the labour market. One way was to give early retirement to older people who had been unemployed for a long time. This and various other methods were used to bring the official unemployment rate down about 5 percentage points.

Now that there is a labour shortage, the employment rate is a better indicator of labour potential, because it measures the proportion of 15-64 year-olds that have a job. It may seem strange that there could be a labour shortage when the unemployment rate is still over 10%, but much of this is structural unemployment - people with the wrong skills or living in the wrong place. Labour mobility is rather high in Finland, but so is structural unemployment.

24.2. WHAT DO DIFFERENT JOBS PAY?
Gross monthly earnings, private sector, in euros, 1996

Hotel chambermaid	1209
Fashion sales assistant	1233
Food sales assistant	1245
Chef	1376
Waiter (fixed salary)	1468
Travel agency clerk	1576
Accountant	1621

Health care operative	*1666*
Head waiter	*1704*
Insurance clerk	*1728*
Bank teller	*1772*
Pharmacist	*1779*
Restaurant manager	*1832*
Teacher	*2226*
Car salesman	*2302*
Insurance junior mgr.	*2779*
Junior bank manager	*2889*
Health care manager	*3058*
Car sales manager	*3215*
Bank manager	*3988*
Insurance manager	*4056*

Take-home pay depends on tax, of course, which is affected by a variety of allowances.

24.3. WHY DO FINNS TALK ABOUT "INCOMES POLICIES" INSTEAD OF WAGES?

Because workers realized long ago that gross wages are only one component of wealth. Two others are taxes and prices: wage hikes count for nothing if the government claws them back or if prices rise. Now there is the additional threat of unemployment: if wages rise excessively, Finnish goods will cost more, foreign competitors will steal their markets and workers will be laid off. The old remedy of devaluation is no longer available because of European monetary union.

The three Finnish labour union confederations are large and institutionalized. This allows them to negotiate as almost equal partners with the employers' federation and the government, on a framework for wages and taxes, known as the incomes policy agreement. Each member union then negotiates individually within these central guidelines. It eliminates the leapfrog effect. Finland's excellent current price competitiveness, and the steady fall in unemployment, are largely thanks to the last two incomes policy agreements, in 1995 and 1997. Both lasted two years and covered well over half of all wage-earners.

24.4. HOW MUCH ARE PENSIONS

The mean pension benefit in 1997 was 865 euros per month. There are two main kinds of pension, the national pension and the employment pension (voluntary pensions are still rare, though increasing). The national pension is paid to people aged 65 or over. Early old age pension is available from the age of 60, but it is permanently less, depending on how early it starts. If granted immediately at the age of 60, the reduction is 30%. If retirement is postponed beyond the 65th birthday, the old age pension it is increased by 1% for each month.

About three-quarters of pension payments are made via the employment pension scheme. This links pensions to wages. The contributions are paid mainly by employers. Most of the money received in contributions is paid out to current pensioners. The pension level is set by law and determines the size of contributions. To survive the baby-boom retirement shock, Finland has to make early pensions less attractive and deregulate the employment pension entitlement, so that it corresponds to how much money is in the pot and how well it has been invested.

Agriculture

Most Finnish farms are located in western Finland. The south is the best area for cereal farming, principally wheat, barley and oats but also some rye. Harvests vary considerably, according to the weather. Animal husbandry and dairy farming is concentrated in the east and north. There is also production of potatoes and sugar beets.

With an average size of 14 hectares of fields, Finnish farms are some of the smallest in Europe. The average size in Sweden, for example, is 37 hectares but only 15% of Finnish farms are bigger than 30 hectares.

There are fewer than 100,000 full-time farmers and their average age is rather high.

25.1. HAS THE EU BEEN GOOD OR BAD NEWS FOR FARMING?

It has been good news for consumers and bad news for producers. But the balance of advantages is probably better today than it was before. The old system of agricultural support was opaque and inefficient, but was held in place by the entrenched position of rural interests in the Finnish political system. EU accession offered a way of breaking out of this straightjacket, and the Common Agricultural Policy, wasteful as it is, marks an improvement.

The old system was successful in only one objective: raising the income of the farming community. Income distribution surveys in the early 1990s indicated that farmers' incomes were rising faster than that of any other group of entrepreneurs, employees or office staff. The objective of controlling production was not achieved, and the objective of stabilizing prices was misleading: it meant protecting producers from seasonal fluctuations, which was done by subjecting consumers to severe fluctuations.

25.2. CAN FINLAND FEED ITSELF?

Self-sufficiency was the mantra of pre-EU policies towards agriculture and is still widely regarded as a worthy target today, although Finland has not been close to it for decades. Production of milk and pork routinely exceeds domestic demand, and beef does too in some years. There has been a large surplus of eggs, but EU membership has cut eggs prices so much that output is rapidly falling. Whether or not the cereal harvest meets domestic requirement depends on the weather each year. The biggest shortfalls are in vegetable and fruit production. Only about 20% of the fruit that Finland consumes is produced domestically.

In Finland the debate about agriculture often equates self-sufficiency in food with the ability of the nation to ride out a crisis. This gives farming a gloss of patriotism. But even if Finland produced all the food it consumed in peacetime, it would be unable to do so during a crisis that choked off imports, because farming and the distribution of food are so dependent on oil. To achieve higher self-sufficiency, for example in fruit, farmers would have to use even more oil. If a trade blockade is thought likely, stockpiling makes better sense that a big agricultural sector.

25.3. DO FARMERS HAVE ANYTHING BUT DISADVANTAGES?

The soil is poor, the growing season is short and the rain generally comes at the wrong time. Finland does have potential advantages but they demand active product promotion, which farmers have been slow to realize. Their attitude to food is still production-oriented: "We make it, you need it, where's the problem?" It does not help that the average age of farmers is high.

The advantages that already exist are not being utilized. Finnish farmers use less herbicide and pesticide than most, because the harsh winter kills pests and disease, but too much is still used. Only 8% of Finnish territory is agricultural land, so farming has little effect on the whole environment, but the amount of fertilizers and animal waste that runs off into rivers and lakes is still excessive. For selling pure goods at premium prices to demanding European consumers, a zero-tolerance approach is needed. And because one rotten apple can spoil the reputation of the barrel, a nationwide approach to marketing Finnish food would be less effective that tightly knit local consortia selling directly to specific European distributors.

25.4. ARE THERE ANY WINES WORTH TRYING?

The number of local wines has increased greatly since EU accession, which cut the power of the state alcohol retailer, Alko, to decide what was worth stocking. Now farms can sell their wines (but not stronger products like liqueurs) directly to the public. About fifty do so. By and large, these wines bear out the original judgement of Alko tasters: they are a mediocre lot that do not stand international comparison. Nor can one talk of Finnish vineyards, because grapes refuse to grow here. Finnish wines are produced from imported grape must, flavoured with Finnish fruit before fermenting.

Of the 120 wines produced in fairly commercial quantities, connoisseurs single out only a handful as worth four stars. These are Aino whitecurrant and Briegu blackcurrant wines from Ilomantsi in North Karelia, J.J.V. Helsten's gooseberry wine from Kirkkonummi, raspberry wine from Leppämäki and cranberry wine from Koivusalo. Of mass-produced conventional wine, Elysée dry sparkling by Marli also gets top points. The Finnish tradition is brewing, not winemaking, and the range and quality of commercial beers reflects this. For rustic adventures there are microbreweries producing traditional "sahti beer" in the triangle Tampere-Lahti-Jyväskylä of southeast Finland.

Forest Products

Finland has only 0.5% of the world's forests but accounts for 5% of its forest industry production. As an exporter it is even more significant because countries like Japan and the United States consume so much of their own output.

The bulk of Finnish forest industry production is sold abroad, generating about a third of export earnings. The mechanical forest industry means sawmills and plywood and board production. The chemical forest industry means pulp and paper. The main trees used are spruce, pine and birch, half to the mechanical side and half to the chemical side. Some wood is imported, mostly birch, which can't be obtained in Finland at a price the industry wants to pay. Recycled pulp is also imported.

26.1. WHO DECIDES ABOUT FELLING AND RECYCLING?

Over 80% of the wood used by the forest industry comes from privately owned forests, so it's the owners who decide. There are about 440,000 separately owned forests, averaging about 30 hectares each. Clear-cutting is still permitted but the average size of clear-cut areas is only 1.8 hectares on privately owned land, which is rather small-scale by international standards. If enough trees are not left to reseed the area naturally, the owner is obliged to plant saplings.

With only 5 million people Finland does not generate a great volume of recycled paper but, after long scorning the idea, the Finnish forest industry woke up to its symbolic importance in the 1990s. By 1997 over 60% of all paper used in Finland was recycled, which is the fifth best rate in the world. (Germany manages some 70%.) Thanks to green Europe's enthusiasm for recycling fibre, it has become a cheap raw material. But some virgin fibre - what the industry calls trees - will always be needed because the pulp steadily deteriorates with every cycle.

26.2. WHY USE SO MUCH MACHINERY?

Despite its enormous output the forest industry employs only 60,000 people and forestry about 25,000 more. This is not much compared, for example, with engineering and electronics, where twice as many people work. It is one reason why paper costs so little. A look round a paper mill shows how it is done: a handful of workers dwarfed by machinery costing at least 250 million euros. The forest industry is very capital intensive.

The same trend is visible in forestry. A tractor-like harvester, which fells a tree at ground level, strips its branches and then cuts it up into standard lengths, works as fast as the 15 men with axes and 50 with saws that it replaces. Wheeled vehicles do cause compacting of the earth, unlike the old horses that worked the forests, so some forest vehicles walk on legs instead of rolling on wheels. And the transportation of wood, which used to involve men dragging great rafts of logs along lakesides, is now done by road. Forest work looked romantic in old Finnish movies but the reality was dangerous, backbreaking, sweaty labour under constant attack from mosquitoes.

26.3. IS PAPER CONSUMPTION GOING TO FALL IN FUTURE?

So far it's still growing at 100 million tonnes a year, though that doesn't mean it will grow forever. The first electronic offices failed to cut paper demand because the software was not sophisticated enough and because their electronic machines were often paper-based, like the fax. Today's networked workplaces obviously use far less paper than they otherwise would.

Yet three trends point to continuing growth of demand for paper. The amount of administrative work continues to grow. Also, large parts of the world, especially in Asia, are reaching the development stage where use of paper convenience products climbs steeply. Finally, degradable renewable forest products are often in better harmony with ecological values than the alternatives. Milk bottles, for example, no longer seem so cute when you calculate the energy needed to transport all that glass, to wash and sterilize them, and then to purify the dirty water.

26.4. HOW DO YOU MAKE PITCH AND TAR?

In the 18th century tar was Finland's big export product, sold mainly to the Britain. Today only a few thousand barrels are produced each year, for use in traditional crafts, cosmetics and confectionery. Tar is made by the destructive distillation of wood. Some is still produced in the old way, though as a hobby rather than a business.

You need a large amount of resinous wood, like pine and fir trunks. Start collecting it a few years in advance. Chop it into equally thick sticks. Next build a tar pit using clay. This is a circle several metres in diameter that is slightly concave, so that liquid will flow to its centre, where it can be drawn off along a pipe. Stack the cordwood in this circle, with the thicker ends outward so that it eventually forms a dome with all sticks pointing to the centre. Cover this with damp turf and light it from the bottom. In the centre the temperature will reach 400 degrees, but the lack of oxygen stops it burning. Draw off the first tar after 48 hours.

Engineering

Although it has now been overtaken by the electronics sector in the value of its output, traditional engineering still provides more jobs. There is also more diversity in engineering: a large number of companies of very different sizes. Conventional subcontracting is giving way to networking and contract manufacturing.

The main products are investment goods required the forest industry, mining and rock crushing equipment, ships, elevators and diesel engines.

27.1. WHY DID ENGINEERING
    SPRING FROM?

The engineering industry did existed before the Second World War but it had a low profile, mainly serving the home market especially the forest industry. Exports began suddenly after the war because of the large amount of reparations payable to the Soviet Union. Finland would have liked to use its forest industry for this, but the USSR demanded that over 70% of the goods must be heavy engineering products, such as ships and locomotives. This demanded large-scale investment. By 1949 engineering output was twice as high as in 1945.

Even as a non-paying customer, the USSR was very demanding. There were strict deadlines for every delivery, a fine was set of 5% per month for any delays and the concept of force majeur was not permitted. Any export department would benefit from such training. Of course, reparations were also an extremely large income transfer and there were great celebrations when the last trainload of goods crossed the border in 1952.

27.2. HOW DOES A PAPER
    MACHINE WORK?

Though invented by the Chinese about 2000 years ago, papermaking wasn't mechanized until the 19th century and wood wasn't used as pulp until about 1850. Until then the main component was rag. Chemically dissolving the wood, instead of just grinding it up, dates from the 1870s. Finland's first paper mills were founded around that time.

Paper starts as a mixture of pulp and water in the headbox at the "wet end" of a paper machine. It is spread evenly on a wire mesh screen, where most of the water drains away. The rest of the machine is to dry it and roll it smooth. The drying section is the longest part of the machine and it needs the most energy, so a lot of research has gone into making it more efficient. The other critical parameter for such expensive machines is their speed.

27.3. DOES SHIPBUILDING HAVE A FUTURE?

There's been shipbuilding in Turku, southwest Finland, since 1737 and the Turku New Shipyard is one of the largest and most modern in Europe. The Helsinki shipyard dates from 1865. The main products today are cruise liners and passenger ships, gas carriers, icebreakers and other special icebreaking vessels. Over the past ten years about a quarter of the world's large cruise liners have come from Helsinki and Turku. Yet people wonder if such a mechanical industry has a place in Finland's future.

It has gone bankrupt before. Masa Yards is what's left

28.1. WHY DO THE COMPANIES HAVE SUCH STRANGE NAMES?

Outokumpu and Rautaruukki were established before the current fashion of inventing corporate names that sound solemnly Latin, like Patria or Mandatum. Rautaruukki just means "iron works". Outokumpu is named after the sleepy town in North Karelia that grew up around its first mine. Headquarters are now just outside Helsinki and the mine is now a local tourist attraction. The name translates as "odd hill".

Nokia has been luckier with its name, eminently pronounceable although it is just as Finnish. It too is the name of the town where it was established, an industrial area near Tampere, central Finland. The famous offspring of that town has moved on but the spun-off Nokian Renkaat (Nokia Tyres) is still there, a reminder of Nokia Corporation's low-tech beginnings.

28.2. WHY MAKE STEEL WHEN YOU DON'T PRODUCE IRON ORE?

Finland is home to the largest manufacturer of steel in the north of Europe. It was established as recently as the 1960s, largely for political reasons. Iron and steel production was something that a self-respecting industrial country ought to have. Also the basic equipment was available from the USSR at barter prices, though getting its environmental impact down was not so cheap and easy.

Yet today it is not only a pioneer in environmental matters but also one of the most efficient steelmakers in Europe. Using imported ore instead of local production made sound commercial sense. Coal is imported, too. There are no subsidies, so operations are distinctly unpolitical. The only secret is high productivity, which is no secret at all. In steelmaking, it seems the biggest advantage is to have no tradition.

28.3. IS THERE REALLY GOLD IN LAPLAND?

The first gold was found there in 1836 and there was a gold rush in 1868, though the number of diggers was never greater than 500. Gold panners - most famously in the River Lemmenjoki - have always been finding little grains and sometimes big nuggets; in 1935 they found one the size of a fist, weighing nearly 400 grams. A lot of people have been attracted by the theory that somewhere is the great shining mother lode.

The Geological Survey of Finland has recorded

131 deposits and significant prospects. One of the most promising seems to be Pampalo, near Ilomantsi, where gold was found in 1994. This is now in test production, but there's a lot of digging to be done, down hundreds of metres, which is more than a man and a mule can take on. For romance, though, there are still panners each summer in the Lemmenjoki National Park.

28.4. WHAT ABOUT DIAMONDS?

Until recently no one thought to look for diamonds. When they did, they found them. Eastern Finland meets the combination of criteria that creates a strong likelihood of diamond-bearing rock. So does a lot of northern Russia, but because of political and legal instability it is not as attractive a prospecting area.

Diamonds are formed in pipes of kimberlite rock. Twenty-five kimberlite clusters have been located in Finland since 1994. The main ones are near the town of Kuopio. So far two have been closely studied and found to contain a considerable number of clear and colourless diamonds.

Electronics

Production of electrical and electronics goods was worth nearly 16 billion euros in1998, a third more than the year before. It is now the biggest industrial sector in Finland, having doubled in size in less than a decade. Exports were worth over 10 billion, an increase of 20%. This sector employs 61,000 people: R&D spending was over a billion euros.

The size of companies ranges from large corporations with a global presence to countless small niche operators. Successful products include mobile phones and other telecommunications equipment, computers, electrical motors and transformers.

29.1. WHY IS FINLAND IN LOVE WITH GADGETS?

A gadget is a device of doubtful value. The motor car (which broke down all the time), light bulb (burned out too fast) and radio (heavy interference) were all gadgets before they caught on. In some places even the fax machine is still a gadget because there's no one else to send a fax to. The same goes for e-mail if no one has a computer, or mobile phones if most owners keep them turned off. So a communications device doesn't just have to function properly. It has to reach a critical mass.

A third of Finland's population uses the Internet on a weekly basis, the highest level in the world, so e-mail and other net-based tools aren't gadgets. And about two-thirds of the population have a cell phone, again a world record. In Finland, more convenient communications devices are starting to make the humble, messy fax machine into a gadget again.

29.2. WHAT'S THE SECRET OF NOKIA'S SUCCESS?

Until quite recently it didn't even look likely. Just before Christmas in 1988 the chief executive of the company, responsible for its massive diversification out of heavy industry, was so depressed that he killed himself. Before the current head of the company was appointed in 1992, two successors had been hired and fired. And the company continued to make losses. Yet by the end of the decade Nokia was one of the most profitable, buoyant corporations in the world.

The management of the company changed radically at the start of this decade. Rarely can a Finnish chief executive get rid of all the cronies of his predecessors. The new men at the top shared a vision of communications products and also about the environment in which they would flourish. As with the PC, the key was a broad standard, which required negotiations and lobbying as well as technical prowess. And work, work, work. Nokia's slogan is "connecting people" but in-house they say it's "disconnecting families".

29.3. IS NOKIA TOO BIG FOR FINLAND?

Nokia produces nearly a fifth of Finnish exports. By some estimates it produces 4% of Finnish GDP. It also dominates the Helsinki Stock Exchange in terms of share value and trading. That's a lot riding on one company and certainly poses a short-term risk. In the longer run, though, the picture is rosy

Nokia is the most visible part of the telecommunications cluster. The concept of growth and prosperity through more efficient communications is solidly established, so the tele cluster is a vital piece of Finland's infrastructure, helping all other sectors of the economy perform better. It's the speed of this new development that's frightening; but it seems inconceivable that telecommunications will lose its importance as quickly as it gained it.

29.4. WHEN EVERYONE'S GOT A CELL PHONE, WHAT NEXT?

Mobile phones are where Nokia makes most of its profit, though it has other divisions. In 1998 Nokia sold more mobile phones than any other company in the world. It has also managed to keep average margins high by bringing out new models before the glamour starts to wear off the old ones. So even after mobile phone penetration reaches 100% (which is a long way off in many countries) it can still go on selling phones if it can keep inventing new applications.

The company is already benefiting from the trend to dual-band phones, which are cheaper to use in city areas. But the real "killer application" is probably going to be the switch to media phones, that will allow web surfing and moving picture transmission in addition to more mundane extras like e-mail, faxing and file transfer. This means genuinely easy e-business and e-banking to every mobile phone owner. Then the information society will reach everyone, not just PC nerds.

Information Technology

Finland's exports of technology were worth nearly 6 billion euros in 1997, compared with 4 billion in 1996. About 18% of all exports are high tech, a high proportion by international standards. The sudden rise of this sector has followed an equally steep climb in R&D spending, now one of the highest rates in the world at 3% of GDP.

There is no single high-tech location like Silicon Valley. The universities, in particular Tampere, Oulu and Helsinki, provide the backbone of technological advancement. Information technology (IT) is a main area. The others include chemistry, manufacturing, energy, construction and environmental technology. Information technology has common applications in public administration, education, commerce, finance, transport, telecommunications, energy and the media.

30.1. ISN'T IT JUST A FANCY NAME FOR DP?

Data processing is at the core of information technology, just as the automobile engine lies behind road transport. But IT also involves integrating different sources of information and then linking them to systems and users. A large part of the work consists of making logical arrangements that work efficiently under a variety of circumstances, rather than just using brute computing power to manipulate words and numbers. In the same way, a successful road transport company pays more attention to logistics than running its trucks as fast as possible.

In early applications of computing, data processing power was used to improve the old tools. In offices, for example, computers were separately incorporated into the typewriter, the fax, the switchboard, the adding machine and the pay slip printer. Much larger improvements in productivity and efficiency result when the old tools are replaced by a system. The foundation is DP but the focus is not on the process but on the result, information.

30.2. WHAT'S THE VALUE OF IT?

The point of information technology is to make existing systems and processes operate better and to make new information services viable. What this adds up to in money terms is not so simple because there are IT operations in most branches of industry and government and an increasing number of applications in the home. Although some specialist IT companies exist, there are also IT departments in the organizations of other sectors.

The figures for turnover and employment are also complicated by the overlap with telecommunications. Nokia, for example, is often mentioned in the same breath at the Finnish IT sector but Nokia not only develops communications solutions but also sells the physical devices, like mobile phones, that they run on. On the leading edge, it is hard to draw a line between system and server. Perhaps the best indicator of IT's value is Finland's extremely high productivity increase in the private sector. Much of this is thanks to IT.

30.3. WHAT IS AN INFORMATION SOCIETY?

A new buzzword, for something that's been around for a long time but is now changing faster than before. The concept of using other people's information took off when man developed language. Information societies had arrived when governments first made schooling compulsory, over a hundred years ago. In the 20th century television brought voluntary adult education, by making new events and visions part of the leisure experience. Today people are realizing they have no choice about lifetime education if they want to keep a job.

Information technology has already moved beyond business and industry to schools, libraries and hospitals. The last holdouts have been the home and the individual. The three keys to storming them are devices, delivery and content. There is a national strategy to do this, and it is actually being implemented. It will probably work, too, because Finns are enthusiastic about new technology. But no one knows how people will actually use this and what lifestyles and businesses it will create. About the future there are only theories, most of them wrong.

30.4. WHY ARE THE FINNS SUCH IT SOPHISTICATES?

A lot of mundane factors came together. Competition in telecommunications is often mentioned, but equally important has been cooperation within the sector and between universities and business, so this is not a simple formula. Universities have played a major role; they have unusually high status throughout society because university education is common. This in turn is because Finnish society has always set great store by education. The tiny minority of children who leave school at sixteen are pitied by their peers; voluntary ignorance wins no points. This quest for learning continues into adult life education. About 40% of employees take part in some kind of extra training each year. A common subject is how to use computers.

The pioneers in using IT were the banks, back in the 1970s, but it did not spread much to other sectors. Then came the great Finnish slump of 1990-1994. Large-scale bankruptcies and 20% unemployment gave a powerful economic stimulus to other businesses and government to get more for less. Hopefully a society doesn't needs this kind of a kick in the pants too often to stay ahead.

Financial

The financial sector has been greatly consolidated in the past few years, thanks to the slump. The savings bank group has practically disappeared, and Finland's two largest commercial banks first merged together and then merged again with one of Sweden's largest. There is strong pressure for innovation.

Insurance companies are also changing their focus, from premium income to investment operations, though at a slower pace. Accident insurance and life assurance generate about the same annual income, just under 2 billion euros. These are dwarfed by income from pension insurance - 4.25 billion - which, in Finland, is largely handled by the private sector rather than the state.

31.1. WHY IS FINLAND OVERBANKED AND UNDERINSURED?

Although there are 342 banks in Finland, there are really just three main forces, Merita, Leonia and OKO, the cooperative bank group. OKO consists of 249 banks, but they are all ultimately responsible for each other's liabilities and commitments. Together these three account for 88% of deposits and loans. The numbers of bank branches, about 1600, and employees, 2600, are still high. The apparent strategy is to avoid upsetting customers with too much change before the bulk of them are willing to make the switch to on-line banking services. This will be soon.

Insurance companies were less shaken by the banking crisis in the early 1990s and have been slower to seek new business and compete for shares of existing markets. However, competition from the banks for life insurance is now stimulating that market.

31.2. COULD THERE BE ANOTHER BANKING CRISIS?

The Finnish banking crisis began in 1991, when SKOP threatened to collapse. The Bank of Finland did not dare allow it to fail because all other major banks were sick, too. By 1995 about 10% of GDP had been spent on keeping them afloat. In a fight for market shares, they had been overgenerous in their lending in the boom years of the 1980s. Capital adequacy was already at dangerously low levels when the slump of 1990-94 slashed the value of loan collateral.

Supervision of banking is considerably stronger today. Merger and failure have reduced the number of banks. Minimum capital adequacy for all banks is 8%, and combined capital adequacy is 11.6%. Another major difference is that Finnish industry and the capital market are no longer so bank-centric. There would be less fallout if a bank did fail.

31.3. ARE THE BANKS BIG ENOUGH YET?

Banking gurus believe the future will belong to a few genuine global giants and a large number of smaller banks with special local advantages. All but one of Finland's banks obviously fall in the latter category. But MeritaNordbanken, formed in 1997 in a merger between Finland's largest and one of Sweden's largest, is too big to be local yet too small to be global. A balance sheet total of nearly EUR 100 billion makes it the biggest in the Nordic countries but still a minnow on the global scale.

MeritaNordbanken believes that a third path is open in the highly developed Nordic area: that of a regional giant. It's looking hard for acquisitions in other Nordic countries. This is a race against time because, even if the future belongs to three types of bank instead of two, one of the emerging global giants will want to buy its way into the Nordic market. A lot of eyes are focussed on Finland's Leonia bank.

31.4. WHERE ARE THE FOREIGN BANKS?

There are only six foreign-owned credit institutions with branches in Finland that are entitled to accept deposits. Their share of lending by foreign banks is about 3% and of deposits only about 2%. This is higher than a few years ago but still not much. They showed more enthusiasm - and local banks were more worried - in the 1980s than the 90s.

The simple explanation is that deposit banking is not very profitable in Finland at present. The margin between lending and borrowing rates is tiny, so retail banking, with all the expense of establishing branches, is not attractive. If there is a foreign surge into Finland it will come in the form of an acquisition but, at present, the ownership of local banks is firmly cemented.

Commerce

Sales of daily goods are controlled by a few large chains, which have closely integrated their purchasing, wholesaling, distribution and retailing. Margins and profitability are comfortable. Franchised entrepreneurs sometimes operate smaller stores, but the scope for independent buying and pricing is tightly restricted. Even specialist shops for domestic appliances are in fact branded subsidiaries of the same chains.

Market erosion by mail order was averted by acquisition of the leading mail order companies. The threat from foreign chains was combated by international partnership agreements. One of the few sub-sectors where entrepreneurs have grabbed the market is in sales of personal computers. Hence the cheapness of PCs in Finland.

32.1. WHEN ARE THE SHOPS OPEN?

Shop hours are controlled in Finland. They may be open from 07:00 to 21:00 Monday to Saturday, and on Sunday in June, July, August and December, as well as five other Sundays, decided separately. The law was relaxed in spring 1997, when the government nearly deregulated opening hours completely, but lost its nerve at the last moment in the face of opposition from the shop workers' union. Kiosks and filling station convenience stores are also happy with the restrictions, because they are exempt.

In a cartel, more freedom to compete does not lead automatically to competition. However, four months after the new law took effect, the main chains decided simultaneously to start keeping longer hours. Previously most were open only until 19:00. One reason for their change of heart was the popularity of the Bold and the Beautiful, shown after 18:00, which had been emptying their shops an hour before closing time.

32.2. WHERE DO THEY HIDE THE WINE?

Not in the food stores. Those bottles of pink and yellow stuff have been doctored to have no more than 4.7% alcohol by weight, so that they can be sold in ordinary shops. As a result, their flavour does not resemble wine. According to the Alcohol Act of 1995, the sale of stronger drink is subject to licensing. In practice, this license is granted only to the state-owned alcohol monopoly Alko. There are a few exceptions, like the permits granted to farms to sell their berry wines, which also bear a little resemblance to wine. For a decent drink of any strength, you must seek out an Alko store.

It will be a pleasant surprise. The range of wines is excellent and so is the price:quality ratio. Alko's strong beers are also good, though hardly cheap. Spirits are downright expensive. This is national alcohol policy. Medium strength beers and ciders, 2.8-4.7% alcohol, can be sold in food stores, though only to those above the age of 18. Beware, also, of the "teen-drinks" - less than 2.8% for those determined to make a early start on the road to ruin - alongside the false wine. Be grateful you weren't in Finland in 1919-1932, when there was total prohibition and only doctors and dentists could legally buy a drink, for medical and scientific purposes of course.

32.3. WHAT ABOUT THE EUROPEAN CHAINS?

Until fairly recently Finland had too small a population and too little purchasing power to interest the big European retailers. Finland's own chains used the time wisely to strike deals with some of the best European brands of clothes and food, selling them here under their own names, or under the foreign name but within the Finnish chain. When outsiders could not be bought off, zoning and other political pressures were used. A Swedish furniture chain managed to buy a plot of land on a plain but busy road east of Helsinki, only to be told that its planned supermarket would disfigure a historic landscape. It took nearly 20 years to get the go-ahead to build.

This protectionism meant a narrow range of arbitrarily priced goods. When Finland joined the EU, middle-class Finns were outraged to hear that food parcels given to the poor would contain olive oil, which was still priced as a luxury good in Finland. Since EU accession, breaking into the Finnish market has been easier but only the Swedes have bothered to try.

32.4. DOES E-BUSINESS HAVE ANY PROSPECTS?

In view of the high density of Internet connections in Finland, it ought to have, but there's not much sign of it yet. Most on-line commerce is still business-to-business. Only a few consumer goods are available, like stamps, computers, books, CDs and flowers. There is nothing original here. The ideas are borrowed from the United States. What makes this inactivity all the more surprising is that Finland has a much more widespread and secure on-line banking system than the US, so the problem of reliability is less. For example, of the entire clientele of Merita Bank, about 40% are on-line customers.

The breakthrough is probably just around the corner, when the new generation of WAP mobile phones will bring ease of use to the Internet and push on-line commerce out into the mass market. It may have been right to wait. As America's pioneers have shown, there is rarely any permanent advantage to being first and you need deep pockets.

Energy

Supply of energy per capita in Finland and Sweden is high, though much less than in the United States and Canada. The reason is not that the Finns and Swedes have to heat their cold northern homes so much but that their forest industries are so energy intensive.

Industry uses nearly half of all energy in Finland, space heating only a quarter. Finland has no fossil fuels except peat. Oil, the main source of energy consumed in Finland, is imported. So are coal, natural gas, and electricity. Hydropower is an indigenous source.

As the economy grows, total energy consumption is rising, electricity the fastest. Condensing power is rather efficient in Finland because of advanced co-generation of electricity and heat.

33.1. WHY NOT REPLACE NUCLEAR POWER WITH HYDROELECTRICITY?

Hydroelectric power stations produce only about 3% of Finland's energy consumption, while nuclear power produces 17%. Finland has four nuclear power units. There are a great many more hydroelectric stations, but they typically produce rather little electricity. Geography is to blame. Norway and Sweden have mountain rivers full of energy. Finland's meander placidly through fields and forests. Taming them to produce electricity involves regulating lake water levels, which upsets lake life, like the seals in Lake Saimaa. In fact hydroelectric capacity has already been exploited beyond reasonable ecological limits.

Nuclear power is important because it works so well. Since 1983 the annual load factors of Finland's nuclear stations have been about 90%, some of the highest in the world, yet with no serious accidents. The public is uncomfortable about the final disposal of radioactive waste but many feel that the short and medium-term alternatives to nuclear power would be worse. There is a rather strong lobby for building another nuclear power station.

33.2. WHAT ABOUT OTHER NEW ENERGY SOURCES?

The most promising candidate to replace imported oil is imported natural gas because it produces fewer emissions. Finland has its own peat reserves but this is a dirty, expensive fuel that can be exploited only at considerable cost to the environment. Now that the trade balance is no longer a cause for concern, it is best forgotten. Wind power is negligible, because most of Finland is not windy, meaning a very large capital investment in building the towers compared to what they yield. And wave power is a non-starter on the Baltic, which is too small to have tidal waves.

An intriguing future form of energy might be liquefied wood. In a process called pyrolysis, wood chips are gasified at a temperature of 500-600 degrees and then the gas is cooled to produce oil. It's the same process as used to make tar (see 26.4) but it's more efficient and faster. Wood oil can be used in burners intended for mineral oil. The ecological attraction is that net carbon dioxide emissions are zero, because the amount emitted when the wood oil burns is exactly the same as the original tree absorbed when it grew.

33.3. SHOULD FINLAND REDUCE ITS EMISSIONS?

At the Kyoto Climate Convention in December 1997, the European Union agreed that, by 2008-2012, its member states will emit 8% less greenhouse gas than they did in 1990. There are six greenhouse gases identified but for the EU the main difficulty is curbing carbon dioxide, produced whenever carbon-containing fuels like coal, oil or gas are burned. And there are other unpleasant emissions like sulphur and nitrogen oxide produced by industry that ought to be reduced because they cause acid rain.

Without a change in energy policies, Finland's economic growth will result in more energy consumption and more emissions. Coal and oil are cheap, so energy utilities would be foolish not to use them. Their price is wrong because it does not reflect all the costs resulting from their use. This is a prescription for new taxes, to push up the cost of cheap-but-nasty energy sources, and to raise incentives for saving energy. Unfortunately the political lobby that loves environmental taxes also hates nuclear power, which produces zero emissions of dangerous gases. If other parts of the EU close down their nuclear power stations without cutting energy use drastically, Europe's emissions will rise so high that it won't matter what Finland does.

33.4. HOW DOES A COMPETITIVE ELECTRICITY MARKET WORK?

Transmitting energy is a natural monopoly because it makes no sense for every electricity producer to lay cables to all consumers. But the Electricity Market Act of 1995 sets the rules for using the power grid, overseen by the Electricity Market Authority. The national grid is no longer owned by a single power company but jointly, by two power companies, the Finnish government and institutional investors. This grid interfaces with Sweden, Norway and Russia, so power surpluses can easily be bought and sold.

Since 1997 individual households have been able to choose which power producer they buy their electricity from. The cable is the same but the origin of the invoice varies and so does the sum billed. Prices have already fallen quite a lot. The situation is still a bit confused because there are more than a hundred electricity distribution companies but, as the number declines, the market should work better.

Transport

There are about four cars in Finland for every ten inhabitants, up from 2.5 in 1980. Their average age is rather high by western European standards, because of the high sales tax on private cars.

As recently as 1950, trains were the dominant form of transport for passengers as well as freight. Following a rapid expansion of the highway network in the 1950s and 1960s, road now carry about 60% of domestic freight, compared with 25% by rail.

There are 78,000 kilometres of public roads. The rail network has been reduced somewhat to 5.8 thousand kilometres, of which about a third is now electrified. The rail service operator, VR, is state-owned. In the past ten years, the number of postal consignments has fallen by 6% and the number of post offices by nearly 50%.

34.1. WHY DON'T HELSINKI BUSES SAY WHERE THEY ARE GOING?

There is not enough room on the front of a bus to indicate its destination in both of Finland's official languages, Swedish and Finnish, in letters big enough to read from afar. In the sensitive politics of language, it is better not to do something at all rather than do it in the wrong way. This is why, instead of names, Helsinki area buses have numbers derived from the postcode of the terminus. Unfortunately few visitors have memorized the postcode directory.

There's been talk of fitting buses with electronic signs that would flash the destination alternately in both languages. In future, it will also be possible to get route and timetable information on the screen of your mobile phone. In the meantime, you have to look at the board above the bus stop, which shows the numbers of the buses that that stop there and their ultimate destination (though not their routes). Doing this quickly before the bus roars past has brought extra excitement to many a vacation.

34.2. ARE THERE RAILWAYS IN FINLAND'S FUTURE?

A century ago a journey in Finland was quite likely to involve a trip by boat or horse. The railroads were build up in the early 20th century, but the low population meant that the network was scanty and many areas remained isolated, a journey of several days from the important centres. It was the rapid improvement in the road network during the 1950s and 1960s that really opened up the country. And then came air travel, to link the main cities. In this respect Finland remains rather different from core areas of Europe, where railways played a key role.

Because of low traffic it has not been worthwhile building direct tracks. Lakes make this problematic anyway. The track to eastern Finland goes northwest first. The route to Lapland skirts the Gulf of Bothnia. Even if speeds are raised, the journey from Helsinki to Rovaniemi is not going to fall much below ten hours. In the far south, rail can be continue to be useful, especially in commuter traffic, but not for long-distance travel, especially since geography and a different gauge isolates the Finnish network from continental Europe.

34.3. WHY ISN'T HELSINKI'S AIRPORT CALLED HELSINKI AIRPORT?

Helsinki has its own airport at Malmi, but it's unsuitable for modern airliners. After the Second World War, planning began for something bigger, but Malmi was then being run by the Allied (Soviet) Control Commission, in charge of supervising Finnish compliance with peace terms, under Stalin's notorious side-kick Andrei Zhdanov. The most suitable alternative site was over the border in the neighbouring municipality of Vantaa, hence the name Helsinki-Vantaa Airport. It was ready just in time for the

Olympic Games in 1952.

There was a lot of construction and development in the late 1990s and, in 1999, it was voted the best airport in the world in a survey by IATA. The only areas where it did not shine concerned Finland's location, an inconvenient place for travel within Europe. The locals, by the way, still call the airport Seutula, the name of the nearest village at the time it was built.

34.4. WHY NOT BUILD A "CHANNEL TUNNEL" TO SWEDEN OR ESTONIA?

From Turku on the west coast to Stockholm is 300 kilometres, which is out of the question. From Helsinki to Tallinn is a more feasible 100 kilometres, though still very expensive. Even a society has been established to promote the idea. Like the channel tunnel between England and France, this would be for rail traffic rather than cars and lorries.

The key questions are whether there will ever be enough freight and passenger traffic to justify such a large investment. It is quite possible that the telecommunications revolution will damp down the trend of increasing traffic. If Estonia were ever linked into a high-speed European rail network, the prospects would look better, but it might still make better sense to skirt the Gulf of Finland via St. Petersburg, an area with a larger population than the whole of Finland. In the meantime, the ships, catamarans and hydrofoils that cross between Helsinki and Tallinn are fast and fun.

Communications

The first telephones were installed in Finland a year after they had been invented and the Finns have been addicted to them ever since. Today 95% of households have at least one fixed line and/or a mobile phone. There are over 40 different telecom operators.

Above four in ten Finns have a mobile phone, using the European GSM standard. The world's first GSM call was made in Finland in 1961.

By some calculations Finland has the greatest density of Internet connections per head of population in the world. More than 20% of the population uses the net at least once a week and 12% do so daily. About half of users have a connection at home and 60% have one at work.

35.1. WHERE DID ALL THE PHONE COMPANIES COME FROM?

Most European countries have one, two or perhaps even three telecoms. Finland has 46. This is an accident of history. When the telephone was invented in the last century, the Russian bureaucrats who then ruled didn't realize its importance. The army controlled the telegraph but as long as phone companies remained small and local, they were ignored. It wasn't until well after independence that the state of Finland set up its own company, Sonera, and it never became dominant. 70% of the population is still served by private, local telephone companies.

Even so, ownership of the physical network has limited the amount of competition. In this respect, the Helsinki Telephone Company is very powerful; doubly so because it also owns the metropolitan network for cable tv, which would otherwise be a rival. But cellular phone subscriptions already outnumber fixed connections and cellphone use will soon be universal. This will bring genuine new choice to the retail telecom market, already experiencing aggressive competition from a major Swedish operator, Telia.

35.2. HOW DID THE MOBILE PHONE REVOLUTION GET STARTED?

Mobile phone use grew through a chain of fortunate, interconnected events. First, because of their small population base, the Nordic countries were the first to realize how important a standard is. The PC revolution took off in the same way, from a standard designed by IBM but, in contrast to the computer business, no single telecom dominated the world. Until quite recently, some bigger countries were still trying to go it alone with proprietary mobile phone systems.

The Nordic Mobile Telephone (NMT) standard dates from 1987. Having seen its benefits, Finnish and Swedish telecoms and their customers immediately grasped the advantages of a common standard for all of Europe, GSM, and changed over after 1992, when this became possible. Because the number of users was already large, the payback time for investments in mobile systems was very short, and Finland's private telephone companies wanted a share of the business. This created GSM competition in Finland from the very beginning, pushing down call tariffs and making the market grow even faster.

35.3. WHY THE PASSION FOR THE INTERNET?

As with mobile phones, the Finns seized onto a standard for linking computers as soon as one became available. Previously the general method for joining university networks was not much different from normal voice telephony. A single circuit was created, linking the two places, and individual bits were sent down the line, one after another. By the mid-1980s it was clear that a new standard, the basis of the Internet, was feasible, reliable and efficient, and the Finnish University and Research Network jumped on board.

Perhaps because university education is so common in Finland, there is close co-operation between universities and business life, especially in technology. The new standard quickly made the jump into the private sector and then into ordinary lives, aided by competition between telecom companies. Government bodies too played a formative role because they realized that Finland had everything to gain from a technology that reduced the significance of geographic isolation.

35.4. ARE THERE ANY SUCCESSFUL INTERNET BUSINESSES?

In 1991, a 21-year-old student at Helsinki University invented the operating system, Linux, that powers most of the world's Web servers. Linus Torvalds still oversees Linux development today, the best-known programmer on the planet and a bona fide celebrity on the Internet. But this is no business because he made Linux into open source programming, free to anyone who wants it.

The Finns have found it as hard as everyone else has to make money from on-line content. In such a small language area, traffic does not support mass advertising sales. The biggest portal, Sonera Plaza, averages about 1.1 million visits a week from 300,000 different visitors, but most content providers get only a fraction of these numbers. Probably the only on-line business viable on current earnings is banking. Finland's biggest bank, Merita, began offering telephone banking even before the Internet and now has services from account management to securities subscription, and from e-commerce payments to electronic signature. Of its active customers today, 40% are on-line. This makes a contribution to profitability because it allows the bank to reduce its number of branches.

Media

There are 26 newspapers published every day and another 26 published five or six days a week. Three-quarters of all newspapers are bought by subscription and delivered to homes. Figures for single copy sales are correspondingly low.

Half of newspaper income is from subscriptions, half from advertising. Total newspaper circulation fell 20% in the 1990s but is still high at 3.3 million. The most popular tv programmes draw an audience of about 1.5 million.

Public broadcasting is subject to license. There are four national television networks. Two are operated by the state-owned Finnish Broadcasting Company YLE and two are commercial. About 40% of households are cabled.

36.1. WHY IS HELSINGIN SANOMAT SO DOMINANT?

The Helsingin Sanomat is the only national newspaper, read in most parts of Finland. Its circulation is nearly half a million and estimated readership is over a million. Its "afternoon edition", the Ilta-Sanomat evening paper, is Finland's second largest newspaper. The dailies of Tampere and Turku have only a quarter of this circulation. Helsingin Sanomat represents a standard of journalistic excellence and responsibility that other print and electronic media compare themselves to. It also has considerably more influence on Finnish politics and opinions than the others do, even tv news.

That said, it is not very innovative or aggressive. It did not beat its only credible rival, Uusi Suomi, into submission: that newspaper, which closed in 1991, was a victim of its own suicidal incompetence in management and marketing. Other publishing houses have been quicker to see the trends - free sheets, colour supplements, on-line versions - but Helsingin Sanomat gets there in the end and then proceeds to do it better than the pioneers did.

36.2. IS THE FINNISH BROADCASTING COMPANY INDEPENDENT?

The national public service broadcaster is fairly independent of commercial pressures, because it obtains three-quarters of its revenue from TV license fees (147 euros for 12 months). Parliament's main concern has been to keep this state-owned company independent of government pressure, so it has been made responsible to parliament. After every general election, the new members of parliament elect a 21-member Supervisory Board to oversee the national broadcaster.

The results have been appalling. MPs mostly elect MPs to the Supervisory Board, which then chooses directors for the company, also largely according to their political affiliations. The Social Democratic Party, Finland's largest, has made a habit of installing former party secretaries as director generals (though the present top man is not). These have to be counterbalanced with the appropriate number of centrist, conservative and leftist directors, who then promote or demote subordinates according to party colour. Although there are also non-aligned executives, politics pervades the organization on most levels. Such independence as the company possesses results from these byzantine forces cancelling each other out.

36.3. WHY ARE THERE SO MANY BOOKS PUBLISHED?

Each year the number of original books published is surprisingly large for such a small country: some 8000 non-fiction books and about 1000 works of fiction (in 1997 an exceptional 1700 fiction books). Most of these are written in Finnish, but a number appear in the other national language, Swedish. Each year also sees the publication of nearly two thousand foreign books translated into Finnish.

How can a market of only 5 million people afford to support so much publishing? The answer is that it is not a very competitive business. As you would expect, book prices are high compared with English or Spanish-language markets. Most Finnish authors don't make much money although half of the books published may break even. Finnish biographies rarely do. The profits have been in art books, educational works and schoolbooks. Publishers have used this money to subsidize the rest.

36.4. WHO OWNS IT ALL?

The 1990s have seen the emergence of three mass media corporations, small by European standards but large for Finland. The international media corporations and dynasties of continental Europe have no foothold. The biggest Finnish group is Sanoma-WSOY, with a turnover of 1.2 billion euros. It owns the country's two biggest newspapers, Helsingin Sanomat and Ilta-Sanomat and the second largest business paper, Taloussanomat. It publishes 19 magazines and about 50% of Finland's books. It also owns a national commercial tv channel and has some cable tv operations. One of Finland's wealthiest families holds more than 40% of the shares.

The second largest is Alma Media. It owns a larger and more successful commercial tv station, as well as a number of radio stations. It is also the publisher of the top circulation business daily in Finland, a successful national evening newspaper and three top provincial dailies. The biggest single shareholder is Marieberg, an associated company of the Swedish media giant, Bonnier. The third largest media corporation is the state-owned Finnish Broadcasting Company, which broadcasts on radio and television. None of these three has substantial operations outside Finland.

Advertising

Well over half of all advertising spending is still in newspapers and free sheets. Television accounts for just 20% despite a vigorous increase in the amount of commercial tv programming. Advertisements in magazines and the trade press generate almost as much revenue, 16% of the total. Spending on radio advertising is less than 4%, because the explosion in the number of radio stations has broken up the market and kept prices low.

The Internet more-than-doubled its revenues in 1998 but still took less than half of a percent of all ad spending. Advertisers remain uncertain about what web surfers will buy. There are signs that the first breakthrough will be in recruitment advertising, mainly by wealthy new technology companies.

37.1. WHAT CANNOT BE ADVERTISED?

Tobacco advertising and sales promotion have been banned since 1978. Initially this proved to be a godsend to the leading cigarette companies because it froze their market shares by preventing publicity for new brands. Tobacco is now a dying industry in Finland. Indirect advertising, such as cigarette brand names on clothes and accessories, is also forbidden.

The ban on advertising alcoholic drink was relaxed in 1994. This marked the end of an era of hypocrisy when the only brewery products that could be advertised were unpopular non-alcoholic beers. These were indeed heavily advertised by brewers who happened to make stronger beers with exactly the same names. Now drink no stronger that 22% alcohol can be promoted, although not in a way that emphasizes "positive effects on social life or health". No one has any idea what kind of advertisement would meet this requirement, so it has been roundly ignored.

37.2. ARE THERE ANY SPECIAL MARKETING RESTRICTIONS?

Bans on tobacco promotions are increasing common in the world, and some countries have even stricter limits on alcohol drinks but Finland does have a few unusual rules for the protection of consumers that routinely trip up foreign companies. Most of these apply to marketing to children or advertising that will affect children even if not aimed specifically at them. The law does not define an age limit but the Consumer Ombudsman takes the line that children younger than 12 have not even started to distinguish between advertising and fact.

Advertisements for products and services used by children can't exaggerate, even as a joke. They must give an explicit picture of quality and size. Children don't understand what brochures are for, so they mustn't be sent them unless their parents agree. The same goes for product clubs. Advertisements must not exploit loneliness, or suggest that the article will assist social success. All this makes it extra hard to use children in ads aimed at children. Finally the context matters. Children's products can't be sold in tv shopping programmes and animated ads must not be used in animated children's programmes.

37.3. WHAT'S WRONG WITH FREE GIFTS?

The Consumer Protection Act says there must be a clear and acceptable connection between a free gift and a product. As a rule a free gift is allowed if it is of obviously little value, but with children the rule is tightened. Collection series can be very attractive so these are banned with food products aimed at children. And advertising must always focus on the main product, not the free gift. The free-gift rule applies to marketing aimed at adults, too. The products must always have an obvious connection. This is a bit vague but the Market Court has taken a tough line, even outlawing free gifts that the consumer is allowed to keep if he returns the product ordered.

And marketing lotteries are out. This means that products cannot be sold with the chance to win a free prize, unless people who do not buy the product have an equally good chance. Naturally, this often defeats the object of the promotion. Coca-Cola was once threatened with a large fine if it repeated the offer of a chance to win a yo-yo by buying Coke, Fanta or Sprite.

37.4. WHO ARE THE TOP ADVERTISERS?

A few years ago food was by far the chief category of goods advertised. The Valio dairy cooperative still features prominently, as do the main shopping chains, but competition between cell phone service providers has been reflected in advertising spending. Another large advertiser is the mobile telephone manufacturer Nokia, though part of its spending is on recruitment announcements. Other categories of spending - vehicles, property, office equipment - are conventional.

Sponsorship is growing but is still not big. The top advertisers averaged only about 200,000 euros each in sponsorship payments in 1998. Sport was overwhelmingly the most popular in terms of money spent, but the increase in sponsorship seems to be benefiting environmental matters and cultural activities, where the money buys more gratitude, so objectives are easier to achieve. Total spending on traditional sports, particularly team events, is expected to decline

Sports

Finns may not be sports-crazed like South Americans but, as in other western nations, there is a sizeable minority devoted to sport and strong media coverage of all main events, at home and abroad.

The first national love is track and field. Athletes like Paavo Nurmi ran Finland onto the map in the 1920s and Lasse Viren is still revered for winning four Olympic gold medals in the 1970s. Track and field is now in the doldrums, with world-class performances being achieved in javelin throwing only.

Soccer may be the world's biggest sport but Finland does not excel at it. The main strengths today are in ice hockey and the Nordic ski events, such as ski jumping and cross-country. In the latter, women such as Marja-Liisa Kirvesniemi (nÈe Hämäläinen) and Marjo Matikainen have a permanent place of honour..

38.1. WHY IS FINLAND POOR IN SOCCER?

Like Swedes, the Finns suffer a climatic disadvantage. Because of the harsh northern winter, soccer is a summer event in Finland, separated by several months from when the rest of Europe plays, so Finnish players tend not to get noticed abroad. And there is a lack of good pitches, because grass doesn't grow well enough.

The traditional theory for why Finland should be so much worse than Sweden, Denmark and Norway is that Finns excel in sports that require strong individual performances rather than team skills. A more pragmatic explanation is that summer soccer has to compete for attention with the national sport, Finnish baseball, which draws bigger crowds. Even so, there has been a recent improvement in Finnish soccer standards, with a number of players signed by league clubs, particularly in the United Kingdom and the Netherlands. This could be a future growth sport.

38.2. WHY IS FINNISH ICE HOCKEY SO STRONG?

Ice rinks are two-a-penny in winter Finland. All the caretaker of a playground has to do is move the snow aside, hose down the area in the middle and wait for an hour. Skating forwards, backwards and sideways is soon as natural as walking for Finnish children. World class players like Jari Kurri and now Teemu Selanne had the best possible start.

Finnish ice hockey teams are well organized and have strong traditions, so success breeds success. National events are well attended. And because ice hockey has a fairly small following in the world, top Finnish players do get noticed abroad, especially in America's National Hockey League. This is an extra monetary incentive for success as well as providing idols for up-and-coming players and teenage girls.

38.3. DO BAD ROADS MAKE FOR GOOD DRIVERS?

Despite all the tax they have to pay on them, the Finns love cars. This is not illogical. It was the development of the road network that opened up Finland's interior and it is still practically impossible to reach many parts of the country in any other way. An automobile is an essential complement for the summer cottage in the country that is part of the national lifestyle.

With low traffic densities, Finnish motorists can still enjoy the pleasure of the open road but snow and ice make winter driving conditions demanding. Also, constant maintenance of remote roads is not economically viable so, even in summer, road surfaces can be treacherous. It's an ideal training ground for motor racing. Rallies, in which Ari Vatanen, Juha Kankkunen and Tommi Mäkinen made their names, may be a team effort but the bottom line is the skill of the man behind the wheel. An extension of this is

Finland's success in Formula One racing, with world champions Keke Rosberg and Mika Häkkinen.

38.4. WHAT ABOUT ALL THE OTHER SPORTS?

There's practically no rugby or cricket. Although the Finns have been European champions in American football, they would be slaughtered in the United States. Tennis is amateur and minority. Golf is a young sport and although there are now dozens of 18-hole courses, few are very good. It's expensive to construct a top class course if it will be unusable for so much of the year. Winter golf across the snow is an entertainment that bears less resemblance to the real thing than mini-golf does.

Despite all the lakes, swimming is not very popular as a sport, probably because it has been so refined in countries without open water that it needs a 25- or 50-metre pool rather than the unstable conditions of nature. The international working class sports of pool and darts have enthusiastic amateur followings but, for the gambling man, nothing beats harness racing. The first trotting races were held in 1817 and today there are 20 first class racetracks.

Sauna

The sauna is a form of sweat bath, with dry air at a temperature of 80-90 degrees Celsius (175-195 F). To increase sweating, water is thrown on the stove.

The people taking a sauna bath are seated naked, or in towels, on tiers of wooden benches, the highest being the hottest. The traditional form, the smoke sauna, has almost died out. It had a fireplace with no chimney, the smoke exiting through a small hole near the roof. These disappeared with the development of new sauna stoves, which have a metal casing and a chimney.

It is common to visit the sauna at least once a week. There are more saunas in Finland than cars, an average of one for every four people. In modern city apartments the sauna is part of the bathroom and is heated by electricity. In the countryside it is likely to be a separate wooden building heated by a wood-fired stove.

39.1. WHAT'S SO GOOD ABOUT GETTING SWEATY?

A fan of sauna would ask: what is so attractive about wallowing in dirty soapy water - that is, having a bath? Perspiration cleans the skin pores of any impurities and softens dry skin. At the same time, the heat relaxes the muscles and reduces muscular aches and pains.

Sauna also has a strong social aspect. Families have saunas together and so do friends. It has also proved to be a good way of building camaraderie between people of different backgrounds, brought together by chance. It breaks down barriers, especially between people who are shy or uncomfortable in a more formal context. Finnish social life is very formal, with the glorious exception of the sauna. Many a business relationship has been forged, not in the boardroom, but on the sauna bench.

39.2. IS THERE A RISK TO HEALTH?

Ten minutes at a time is enough for most people but even if you spend as long as twenty minutes in 90°, your skin temperature will still be only about 40°. It is the very process of sweating that holds it down. The temperature of inner organs changes hardly at all. Children have less ability to tolerate heat because they have little fat and a lot of surface area compared with body mass, so they shouldn't have such long, hot saunas as adults. Everyone should leave the sauna room when they feel like it. There are no norms.

Sauna should be avoided by anyone with a fever, or inflammatory diseases. For the rest of us, the biggest systemic shock is if you plunge straight from a hot sauna into cold lake water. This is a macho thing but, if you are in fair health, it evidently does no harm. It is not recommended to people with heart disease, high blood pressure, asthma or skin disease.

39.3. DON'T PEOPLE FIND NUDITY EMBARRASSING?

There are places where an exposed female ankle or mouth is a shocking affront to decency. Other people have come to focus on more narrowly defined areas that must be covered by shorts or bikinis. The confusion of nudity with sex has long traditions. The public baths of Europe, common since Roman times, were ordered closed in the 15th and 16th centuries because of widespread promiscuity and epidemics of syphilis. It was only in the remote areas such as northern Russia, Estonia and Finland that the pure bathing habit continued.

Family sauna in Finland means just that: man and wife and small children. Sauna between friends usually means between friends of the same sex. Indeed, one of the complaints of women in business is that they are shut out of the place where the real deals are made. Sauna in plenty of towels is one solution.

39.4. WHAT IF YOU DON'T HAVE YOUR OWN SAUNA?

This used to be no problem, even in towns. Public saunas were kept permanently hot, men and women being served on different days or at different times. They were run as businesses, financed by a small entrance fee. Also, many apartment buildings had their own saunas in the basement. Alas, when townsfolk started building saunas into their bathrooms, these venerable institutions died out.

But the new generation is used to eating out, drinking out and dancing out, and public saunas are enjoying a revival. In Helsinki, for example, a venerable public sauna has recently reopened (Harjutorinkatu 1) with two wood-heated saunas, massage, a washer and even traditional bloodletting. For more of a party, there is a sauna bar (Eerikinkatu 27) and a sauna café (Töölöntorinkatu 7) in the downtown area.

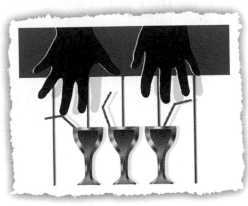

Fun

The special etiquette of urban life is confined to Helsinki, Tampere and Turku. One remaining unusual feature is traditional dancing, especially the waltz and tango. Alcoholic drink can be bought in restaurants by people who have reached the age of 18.

Wine is overpriced, at least twice the cost of the same bottle retail. Draught beer comes in two strengths; "No.3" is up to 4.7% alcohol by volume and "No.4" is stronger. ("No.1" is virtually alcohol-free and "No.2" does not exist.) The basic measure for spirits is 4 centilitres Except where specifically forbidden, smoking is allowed in restaurants.

Dress standards are relaxed, though some establishments require a tie and jacket from men.

Concerts are reasonably priced and so, even, is opera. There are free outside concerts in summer. Cinemas show films in original languages, with subtitles in Finnish and Swedish. The symbols K-8, K-12, K-16 etc. show the minimum age for admission.

40.1. WHAT DO THE FINNS EAT AND DRINK?

If pizzas, hamburgers or kebabs are not available, and there is no nearby Chinese or Italian restaurant, Finns can be induced to eat simple Finnish dishes. The best known are cabbage rolls (minced meat wrapped in cabbage leaf eaten with lingonberries), fish soup (especially salmon soup served with rye bread), meat soup (beef slowly simmered with vegetables) and meatballs (though Swedes believe the recipe was stolen from them). Those with tougher palates may risk the lenkkimakkara sausage, which deposits a thin layer of grease on one's teeth, or pea soup, which is supposed to be eaten on Thursdays only.

In finer restaurants the menu reflects the reason. In summer try the whitefish with new potatoes. Crayfish come into season at the end of July, an expensive excuse for drinking the accompanying neat vodka. In the autumn the menu contains game and a great range of mushrooms. Fish continues to be available in the winter, caught in nets drawn between holes in the sea ice.

40.2. HOW MUCH TO TIP?

A service fee is always included in restaurant prices so a tip is only merited for exceptional service and should not be more than about 5%. In smaller restaurants, a kind comment about the food will be appreciated as much.

The exception is the coat check attendant or doorman, whose salary is probably based on the assumption that each entrant will pay him something. This fee is almost always fixed and displayed, and varies between 5 and 10 markkas. In rougher establishments, where the clientele's creditworthiness is in doubt, you may be asked for payment on entry. Diners in finer restaurants can ask to have the doorman's fee added to their bill for the meal, so that it too can be paid by credit card.

Taxi drivers are not tipped in Finland. Anyone who rounds up the fare when giving change is trying it on, and should have his arithmetic corrected.

40.3. WHAT ARE THE RULES FOR VISITING TO A PRIVATE HOME?

A visitor on a longer stay may be rewarded with an invitation to come to the family home, if only for the solid economic reason that eating out can be pricey. The gift of a bunch of flowers or a bottle of wine will be appreciated; anything more may embarrass. The first ritual is to shake hands with everyone, even children. After a couple of hours it is tactful to mention other engagements and to leave unless the hosts seem seriously upset.

Smoking in private homes is now rare, and even an addicted host is likely to do this on the balcony or in the garden. Dress is usually informal, invariably so if one is invited to a summer cottage for a day or so. Expect very rudimentary facilities with no running water, flush toilets or electricity and come prepared to participate in walking, rowing, fishing, chopping firewood and preparing food because there will be little else to do. A good book for evenings is also a wise precaution.

40.4. WHERE IS SANTA?

Santa Claus has a concrete presence in Finland and is not merely an invisible figure who slips in to deliver presents when everyone is asleep. Parents will often hire a student or other seasonal worker to dress up in costume and beard and deceive their young offspring at the Christmas Eve party. Bookings earlier in the evening are preferred as some Santas lose verbal and motor skills after toasting a large number of different parties.

Naturally the real Santa would not. He lives at Korvatunturi, a mountain beyond the Arctic Circle in Lapland. Access to the area is restricted to the elves but the Finnish Tourist Board, Finnair and a number of other organizations in Lapland and Finland claim to have a special relationship with him. There is even a giant underground theme park named after him at Rovaniemi, the capital of Finnish Lapland.

An international survey in 1998 concluded that the Norwegians were the most sexually active Nordic people, claiming an average of 100 acts of intercourse a year. The Finns, Swedes and Danes were all about the same with 85-88 times so perhaps the difference is explained by Norwegian methodology.

In Finland single people living together claimed to make love 132 times a year while married couples were satisfied with 109. The most sexually active age group is apparently 20-29. They also have the most abortions, about 14 a year per thousand women.

The number of teenage pregnancies and abortions has steadily fallen since the mid-1970s and incidence of venereal diseases has also declined.

41.1. ARE NORDIC PEOPLE SEX-CRAZED?

Nowhere near as mad as the puritans of the world, to single out just one group that is preoccupied with sex. Sexual education and behaviour in Finland and Sweden is almost dispassionate. Public health care services and counselling are available to everyone, with the first contraceptives (IUDs and pills) given free of charge. Every 16-year-old is mailed a booklet about dating, human relations and family planning including, of course, a sample condom. And yet the number of teenage abortions is tiny by international standards and the number of unwanted pregnancies has fallen so much that there are far fewer babies up for adoption than couples on the waiting list.

Nor is promiscuity increasing. Young people start sexual activity no younger than before and the great majority of 15-year-olds are still inexperienced, "completely inexperienced" according to surveys, though perhaps that is an exaggeration. Some researchers say they see signs of more voluntary celibacy among the young. In any case there is no evidence that early sexual education promotes early sexual experience: rather the reverse.

41.2. WHAT ABOUT PAID SEX?

Sex without affection for economic advantage has always existed but it used to be well hidden behind doors and curtains. Only after the collapse of the Soviet empire did the ladies in fishnet stockings and extra-short skirts start arriving in Helsinki and making guest appearances in rural hotels. Many are apparently tourists from St. Petersburg taking an extended, laid-back holiday. To judge from the reaction there was much pent-up demand. The typical city client has generally consumed too much alcohol to be attractive to an unpaid partner. In depopulated rural areas, the tale is more of loneliness.

Selling oneself is not a crime in Finland but holders of tourist visas must not work. Pimping is a crime, so restaurants prefer not to attract prostitutes, especially since the alcohol board tends to cancel the liquor licences of establishments where there are "frequent disturbances". This has pushed the trade out into the streets and into the classified columns of newspapers. Advertised offers of "afternoon company for coffee" are unlikely to involve coffee.

41.3. HOW MUCH AIDS IS THERE?

Few Finns contracted HIV before the disease was identified, perhaps because the gay scene was so subdued then, and a rapid deployment of sexual education managed to stop HIV spreading. Only 70-90 new HIV infections are discovered each year. With so few carriers, considerable resources can be devoted to their care. For example, although several HIV-positive women have given birth, medical precautions have ensured that no babies have been born infected.

This calm could now be shattered by an outbreak of

HIV among intravenous drug users, women as well as men. Throughout the 1980s Finland was well behind the rest of Europe in drug use, but EU accession brought new contacts with southern European ways and the rise of east European crime opened new channels of supply. Just when the general public feels the battle against AIDS has been won, the police warn of a new wave of drug users. Unfortunately they have been direly warning about drugs for twenty years and the impact has worn off.

41.4. WHERE CAN I HAVE A GAY TIME?

Although it is not enough to get you elected, being gay in Finland is no longer enough to prevent it. In Finnish society, gay public officials are a sure sign of acceptance. The change has taken place in just 15 years. This is no longer a hostile environment for homosexuals and there are clubs and bars to prove it. Nightlife is not strictly segregated between gay and straight establishments although there are several places where attendance is a definite statement. Appropriate listings and classified ads appear in the leading Helsinki free sheet, "City", which has occasional issues in English.

People needing special advice should contact SETA, the Finnish National Organization for Sexual Equality, which also publishes an on-line guide to Gay Helsinki.

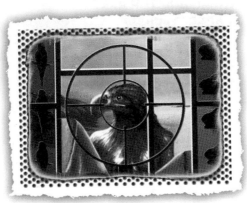

Hunting, fishing

There is no closed season for rainbow trout and other introduced species but most waters close after 10 September because all autumn-spawning trout, char and salmon are off-limits from 11 September to 14 November. Many lakes and rivers have large populations of whitefish, hard to catch but good eating. The season for hunting waterfowl is 20 April to the year-end. The season for marine waterfowl is from the start of September. Moose (Alces alces) the last Saturday of September to 15 December. White-tailed deer (Odocoileus virginianus) the last Saturday of September to 15 January. Hare from 1 September to end of February. Capercaillie (Tetrao urogallus) 10 September to 31 October.

42.1. WHERE ARE THE BEST PLACES TO FISH?

There is a great variety of fish in the lakes and the sea. The salt content of the sea is so low that freshwater species like the perch and pike can be caught there, alongside sea fish like the cod and flounder. Fishing takes place all the year round, even through holes in the ice in winter. A favourite spot for old men in Helsinki is the road bridge leading to Lauttasaari island; great schools of small but tasty Baltic herring rush back and forth beneath it, snapping at any lure. The fisherman doesn't even get his feet wet.

Fishing in Finland can be strenuous or relaxed, fly fishing in the rivers all day or simply dropping a fish trap in among lake reeds and rowing back four hours later to see how big a pike it's caught. For the sportsman even short rivers are generally connected to a nearby lake, from which they are constantly replenished with new fish.

42.2. IS THERE A FISHING LICENSE?

Pole angling and ice fishing are free for all. No licence is required, unless one is river fishing with bait for trout and other members of the salmon family. Ice fishing doesn't even require a pole; just a spool attached to a short stick.

If you are over 17 a license is needed to fish most still waters with a rod. Finland is divided into five large districts, and the same license is good anywhere within the same district. It costs 25 euros for a year or 6 euros for seven days. You obtain it by paying the fee in a bank or post office. (This does not apply to the Åland Islands, where there are different local rules.)

For game fishing, you must first obtain a fishing card, good for one year or seven days, by paying the government's small fisheries management fee at a bank or post office. For each fishing place, such as a stretch of river, you then need a separate permit from the owner. Prices are usually 5-20 euros a day.

42.3. HOW CAN I GO AFTER ELK AND REINDEER?

Hunting rights belong to the landowner, and in southern and central Finland most land is privately owned. For tourists a guided hunting trip is easiest but Finnish enthusiasts join local hunting associations and guest memberships for visitors can be arranged. The permit issued by the landowner or association allows hunting with a local guide only. Hunters must wear an orange hat and coat (for their own protection, not the elk's) and there are tight restrictions on rifles and ammunition permitted. In addition the hunter must have a Finnish hunting license, costing 20 euros, which is issued only after passing a test. A foreigner can avoid the test if he proves he has a licence in his own country.

As for hunting reindeer, you can't. They are domesticated animals and their owners don't like it. They are no challenge anyway. Even if you hit one by accident with your car, you are not allowed to carry it back home to your freezer.

42.4. WHAT CAN YOU DO ABOUT MOSQUITOES?

There are mosquitoes all the year round but warm weather and summer rain gets them moving and makes them hungry. Still water is where they breed and Finland has nearly 50 different species, although just five of them bite people. Judging from their stings they are more poisonous in the spring that later in summer. Gnats are the bane of summers in Lapland and the only thing is to get used to them. Elsewhere a few precautions can reduce the annoyance.

Short sleeves and bermuda shorts are not suitable for walks through the woods. Lotions are available that will repel mosquitoes, but do not suit everyone's skin. Sweat and body odour attracts them, so frequent dips help. Some say that the skin of cigarette smokers is less tasty to them, though this is hardly a reason for taking up the habit. In any case, smoke does drive them away. And make sure that your bedroom/hut/tent is free of them, so that you will be rested and refreshed when you face them again tomorrow.

Touring

The best hiking or trekking season begins in May, or June in the north, and lasts till September. There are wilderness huts along northern trails, available free of charge. Most have unlocked doors, basic bunks and cooking facilities. Some of the easiest walking areas are in North Karelia. There is canoeing and boating at sea and on the lakes.

The islands off the south and southwest coast are ideal for inhabitants of Helsinki and Turku who are rather far from lake areas, but navigation is harder than on inland waters. Sailboats can be rented at 1000 euros a week upwards, depending on the season. Motorboat rentals are 1200 euros per week upwards. Hotels, campsites and youth hostels rent out bicycles at 5-15 euros a day or 42-80 a week.

Bicycles can be taken as luggage on all trains except the high-speed Pendolinos.

43.1. WHAT IS "EVERYMAN'S RIGHT"?

The concept of everyman's right is a traditional code of practice that has evolved in a country where there are few people and a lot of territory. It means that every is entitled to go where they want on land or water so long as they don't intrude on the privacy of others, cause damage or leave litter behind them. Rowing, canoeing and sailing are rarely restricted anywhere, though use of motor boats often is. Mushrooms and berries can be gathered freely in the forest. You can even pitch a tent in wilderness areas, though you must not light a fire without permission from the landowner. There are other restrictions in nature protection areas.

The stipulation of privacy means that you must skirt areas where cottages have been built. Driving off-road is not included in everyman's right, because it damages the land. Sometimes access changes according to the season: in winter you may ski straight across a frozen field but when it is planted in summer you must walk around. Everyman's right applies to people, not dogs, which must be kept under particularly strict control from March to August, when wild animals are rearing their young.

43.2. WHAT'S THE BEST WAY TO SEE THE COUNTRYSIDE?

To see the maximum amount nothing beats private transport. The rail network is too sparse to cover much of the country and goes as straight as possible, so much of the view is just trees or railway cuttings. Roads skirt lakes and get you to the heart of scenic areas but long-distance buses spend a lot of time in town centres which all look alike. Only with a car or chartered coach are you free to see what you want and stop where you will.

Car rental is expensive because of the high price of cars in Finland. Petrol is not cheap either, particularly compared with countries outside Europe. At least parking is no problem apart from in the capital. Road conditions are generally good, especially the motorways that quickly get you away from the dull scenery surrounding Helsinki. Foreign visitors who do not have an EU driver's licence will need an international driving permit, available from an automobile club in their home country. Information about driving regulations can be obtained from Finland's main automobile club, Autoliitto.

43.3. HOW DO YOU AVOID HITTING ELKS?

The elk warning signs by roadsides are not quaint: these large shy animals that roam the forests are deadly on the roads. An adult elk weighs 300-400 kilos and its long legs mean that most of its weight impacts at windscreen height. The fencing alongside main roads is not always enough to keep elks away. Although scared of people they have no fear of cars and will stand motionless and almost invisible in the path of one fast approaching. They cause hundreds of accidents a year, some fatal.

The first rule is to slow down whenever you see elk warning signs, or when driving in poor visibility, and to watch the hard shoulder of the road for any movement. Elks ignore horn honking, and headlight flashing just seems to mesmerize them. If you need to drive round one on the road, go slowly and behind it, because elks won't generally back away. It's also worth remembering that they move in twos or threes so, if you see one, there are more about.

43.4. WHAT ARE THE BEST PLACES FOR CYCLING?

The metropolitan area has an excellent new network of cycle paths and tracks that are generally separate from the road. These soon stop as you cycle away from Helsinki, Espoo and Vantaa, and cyclists are at the mercy of fast cars and lorries on not-very-wide roads. Better to take the fastest route to better cycling territory by loading your bicycle onto a train, bus and boat.

Finland's most popular cycling route is the Åland archipelago, in the far southwest. Roads are flat but varied, with a rich variety of scenery, plenty of water and short distances between interesting stops. Cycle routes are well marked, too. The islands off Turku make a pleasant route, too, combined with ferry trips.

The roads are not so peaceful around the central Lake Päijänne or in the east through the Saimaa lake district but the scenery is magnificent. Quieter cycling is available in North Karelia but it's a longer haul from Helsinki. If you are stuck near the capital, the old King's Road offers a range of old manor houses and churches.

Cruising

The best way to see the water is from the water. Boats leave Helsinki Harbour all through the day in summer to visit the island fortress of Suomenlinna, tour around the local archipelago or head for other towns or countries. There are boat routes down Lake Päijänne and other cruises in the Saimaa lake district on old steam-powered vessels. Most have some catering facilities and some have on-board accommodation, so a full day's journey to another town doesn't necessarily involve seeking a hotel.

In winter the port town of Kemi in Lapland offers excursions out into the frozen wastes of the Gulf of Bothnia. The Sampo, formerly a commercial icebreaker, crunches off into the sea from the middle of December to the end of April. The trips last four hours.

44.1. WHAT CAN YOU
SEE AT SEA?

The archipelago along Finland's southern coast is magnificent. Some islands are no more than a rock and a bush. Others are thickly forested. Channels and coves run in all directions. This is what makes Helsinki and Turku amateur yachtsmen such fanatics and why they pay so much to keep a boat that can't be used for half the year. The cheap alternative is to take a cruise. Some of the islands are inhabited and are linked by scheduled boat traffic during the summer. Tourists can take the round trip.

A traditional cruise from Helsinki is on the old J.L. Runeberg, built in 1912. It departs from the South Harbour and sails east to the old town of Porvoo, stopping at the islands of Svarta Hästen and Pörtö. The trip takes about four hours, the scenery is good and the town of Porvoo is worth seeing too. Beware of going on a Saturday or Sunday, as most of Porvoo will be closed when you arrive. Return either in the same way or by train or bus. Another option is to take your bicycle on the boat there and ride back (50 rather dull kilometres).

44.2. WHERE ARE THE BEST
LAKELAND CRUISES?

For those in the capital with limited time, the "Poet's Way" takes just one day - you're back in Helsinki after about 13 hours. The morning train takes you to

Hämeenlinna, where you pick up the boat to Tampere, Finland's second largest city. The return to Helsinki is again by train. This is tourism rather than leisure cruising but is the fastest way to experience the inland waterways.

If you have the time, you will see more open water on a cruise from the town of Lahti. A bus or train gets you there from Helsinki. There is a choice of cruises. Choose Heinola to be back the same day. To enjoy great Lake Päijänne - and some ten hours on the water - go to Jyväskylä, central Finland. You'll arrive in the evening so accommodation needs to be booked in advance.

Lappeenranta is a good place to start a cruise on Finland's largest lake region, Saimaa, but it's 220 kilometres by road from Helsinki and rather more by rail. A cruise of any length - for example to Savonlinna - has to be part of a plan for several days.

44.3. WHAT ABOUT THE SAIMAA CANAL?

Finns dreamed of linking their biggest lake region to Vyborg on the Baltic Sea for hundreds of years, before finally building the first canal in the middle of the 19th century. Saimaa is 76 metres above sea level. Traffic was halted after the Second World War, when Russia seized much of Karelia. The canal was rebuilt by the Finns on territory leased from Russia in the 1960s and intended to serve as a cheap highway for carrying heavy cargo like wood and ore. With eight locks it cost much more than expected and was a commercial failure.

It's still fine for cruising. Passage normally requires a Russian visa, but visitors on day tours from Lappeenranta to the now-decrepit town of Vyborg need only a passport if their home country has diplomatic relations with Russia.

44.4. WHERE CAN I GO SWIMMING?

Just about everywhere. Lakeland water is usually warm by July. There are other lakes, ponds and rivers everywhere, most of them fine for swimming. There is no concept of trespassing in Finnish law. If you do no damage to the land and keep away from habitation, you can walk and swim where you like.

Helsinki is particularly kind to swimmers all year round. There are several excellent large indoor pools, one of them deep underground. Outside the city is a large water park that is covered and usable in winter. In summer young people head for the swimming stadium, near the Olympic stadium. There's also the sea, unpolluted in most bays of the city and sheltered enough to be warm. Top with sunbathers is Hietaniemi bay, a large sandy beach to the west of the centre. The 55A bus takes you there in 10 minutes from the railway station.

Traditions

The Kalevala is Finland's national epic and colours all images of how life used to be. The roots of the culture it describes stretch back at least two thousand years. It was handed down by rune singing, and the variations and improvisations of different generations have created a fluid timelessness.

Until the turn of the 20th century, rune singing was very important at Karelian wedding ceremonies. These runes were collected by Elias Lönnrot and published in an edited version called the Kalevala in 1835. This poetry is not divided into verses. Instead it consists of chains of line pairs in a distinctive metre. The melody was very narrow and the most common rhythms were 4/4 and 5/4.

45.1. WHEN DID CHRISTIANITY ARRIVE?

According to tradition, the greatest god of the early Finns was Ukko. Christian civilization is said to have arrived in Finland in 1155, with the first crusade from Sweden, lead by King Erik and Bishop Henry of Uppsala. Henry stayed on and met a martyr's death at the hand of a pagan chief, Lalli, on the ice of Lake Köyliö in 1156. By 1296 Pope Boniface VIII wrote of Henry as a saint and he was gradually adopted as the protector of the Finnish church and people. His remains were removed to Turku Cathedral in 1300.

In fact, Finland had been receiving Christian influences from about 1050 onwards, from the Orthodox east as well as the north of Germany. The first "crusade" was a small missionary expedition and was not very successful, because two more were needed to fix Finland in the Swedish sphere of influence. Up to about 1100 Sweden was probably the weaker country and the Finns certainly raided it on several occasions. The glorification of the "crusades" was to give legitimacy to Sweden's growing strength.

45.2. WHAT IS A PELIMANNI?

It's the word for a Finnish folk musician and the style of agrarian music that appeared alongside rune singing in the 17th and 18th centuries and replaced it in the

19th. It came to Finland from Sweden. Initially the most popular kind of pelimanni music in both countries was the polska, a kind of reel, generally played on the fiddle. The most common pelimanni bands consisted of fiddles and a clarinet.

Towards the end of the 19th century the accordion began to catch on, though purists long looked down on it. The Finnish folk music revival seems to date from the first Kaustinen Folk Music Festival in 1968, and it has been strongly in fashion since the 1980s. In 1983 the Sibelius Academy founded a folk music department, the ultimate accolade.

45.3. HOW DO YOU PLAY A KANTELE?

By plucking it. The kantele is a stringed instrument like a zither that was widely played among the people of the Baltic area (kannel in Estonian, kokle in Latvian, kokle in Lithuanian). It consists of a triangular sound box with strings running across it, usually tuned to a diatonic scale. When plucked it makes a sound like a bell.

According to epic poetry the first was made from hair and the jawbone of a pike. Early versions had only five strings and were used to accompany the singing of poems and tales. Designs have become more complex since then, and the number of strings has increased. A concert version, in which the pitch can be changed with a lever, was invented in the 1920s. Larger kanteles have up to 36 strings and are very hard to play. The skill was nearly lost in the 1950s but there has since been a revival.

45.4. WHY ARE THERE SO MANY CHOIRS?

There is a lot of enthusiasm in Finland for choirs, though not as much as in neighbouring Estonia. The explanation lies in the difference between the two countries. For both, song festivals have been an expression of national independence, identity and language. Finland achieved these back in the 1920s. Estonia could not reassert its until the 1990s, after the collapse of the USSR.

With their religious roots, choirs almost died out in Finland after the Reformation but enjoyed a revival in the nineteenth century following the spread of German ideas about song as enlightenment and singing as an aesthetic experience. Finnish nationalism co-opted choir singing as an expression of unity. After independence the unity ended as the nation became politicized, and separate choirs were established for workers. At least the tradition was retained, to flourish still in today's less polarized times.

Music

Interest in art music has increased greatly in the past 20 years. This has had much to do with growing national wealth and leisure, but the Finnish Broadcasting Company has also played a role in helping composers and performers reach a wide audience.

There are now nearly 30 symphony orchestras, as well as regional operas in eleven towns. Finnish musical education is said to be of a high standard. Certainly a large number of Finnish conductors hold posts abroad. Finnish singers have also been well received internationally.

An arts grant system allows composers to concentrate on creative work. Grants are available for one, three or five-year periods.

46.1. WHAT MADE SIBELIUS SO SPECIAL?

The musical career of Jean Sibelius (1865-1957) began in the 1890s, which was lucky timing. Finland was under Russian control and the intelligentsia were discontented. His early works were inspired by epic Finnish tales and the composer rose on the wave of nationalism. His achievement was to rise above national origins. His symphonies pursued a universal style that would transcend borders and barriers, and take him ever further from Finnish roots. His music remained elitist but was never introverted.

Not all nations have acclaimed him: French and Germans have tended to regard him as a minor National Romantic. His work was uneven; he wrote too much for the piano, which he admitted disliking. And in the 1926, when his skills were at their peak, he was beset by self-criticism so merciless that he retreated into silence, though he lived another 30 years. Yet in his brief period of composition, he carried classicism into the modern era.

46.2. AREN'T THERE ANY OTHER FINNISH COMPOSERS?

The boom that Sibelius set in motion, and the national romanticism that he deserted, nourished a great number of careers. At least this cannot be said of the German-born Fredrik Pacius, an example of Germany domination of Finnish music before Sibelius. The Finnish national anthem is not the best of his works but many others had tried to set Runeberg's poem to music with far worse results.

Perhaps the most enjoyable composers apart from Sibelius are those whose styles are farthest from him, like Oskar Merikanto (1868-1924), all-round pianist, conductor, composer and critic who even composed a march for his favourite restaurant, Helsinki's Kappeli. He is better remembered for his Midsummer Night's Waltz. Other notables are Aarre Merikanto (1893-1958), Leevi Madetoja (1887-1947), and Toivo Kuula (1883-1918). Everyone says the young Kuula would have achieved even greater things if he had avoided an argument with a soldier at the Vyborg Seurahuone restaurant amid Mayday celebrations in 1918, and getting himself shot dead.

46.3. IS OPERA POPULAR ENOUGH TO PAY ITS WAY?

Of course not. As everywhere else, it survives on government support and corporate sponsorship. It is more popular than in many countries, and continues to attract talented composers as well as performers, but no audiences would be willing to pay the extraordinary costs involved in an operatic production. For every 50 euros paid at the box office, at least 100 more are needed in subsidies. Opera directors everywhere live hand-to-mouth. When the new Helsinki Opera House was finally ready there was no money left to pay the staff. But something always turns up.

The Savonlinna Opera Festival is therefore a double achievement, not only attracting an audience of 60,000 for each year's month-long season but also mustering the heavyweight corporate sponsors (sorry, partners) that makes it possible. This is opera as tourism, business and entertainment all rolled into one.

46.4. WHO ARE THE TOP OPERATIC SINGERS?

Jorma Hynninen, baritone, has been gathering acclaim for a quarter of a century. He likes romantic roles but audiences prefer him bloodthirsty and mad. Off-stage he is said to be calm.

Matti Salminen's voice has been described as the finest, darkest bass of our time. A big man with a natural manner, he started as a popular singer of tangos.

Soile Isokoski is a soprano whose career has moved quietly since her solo debut in Finland in 1986. Her lyrical voice has grown steadily in strength and character.

Monica Groop is described as an elegant singer, a mezzo-soprano who exudes simplicity. "On the opera stage the clichés are too big," she once said.

Karita Mattila is the volcanic one, a soprano of bold gestures and a monumental personality. More than her peers she lives the life of a jet-setting diva.

Literature & Films

The Finnish novel could not be born until Finnish became the language of the educated classes, in the 19th century. The first practitioner was Aleksis Kivi, who is best remembered for Seven Brothers, a comedy about the clash between peasant values and modern society. Realism and naturalism arrived in Finland in the 1880s, exemplified by Juhani Aho and Minna Canth.

Another early woman novelist, Maria Jotuni, painted satirical pictures of society. F.E. Sillanpää became the only Finn to win a Nobel Prize for Literature in 1939, but he was outsold many times over by Mika Waltari, a natural storyteller who wrote detective stories, film scripts and great historical dramas. Sinuhe the Egyptian has been widely translated.

47.1. IS CINEMA POPULAR IN FINLAND?

Until about 1996 the answer was no. Television was obviously killing it and, when Finns went to the movies, they wanted to see the top foreign titles. Only a few sure-fire local comedies could pack a cinema theatre. The distribution chains responded with heavy investment in the main population centres. The neighbourhood cinema was dead. Cinema-going was to be part of an evening out, not a rival to the television but the complete opposite. The renovations of the Tennispalatsi complex in Helsinki alone cost some 4 million euros, quite a gamble where there were so many competitors.

So far it is working. Cinema visits are about 30% up in 1999, compared with the year before. What's more, the market share of Finnish-made films has suddenly risen, too. There's no explanation for this yet, so it's hard to tell if this is only a temporary phenomenon.

47.2. DO FINNISH FILMS MAKE MONEY?

The market share of Finnish films will have to rise greatly and permanently before they stop making losses. There are virtually no exports, so production is entirely dependent on the home market. About ten full-length films are made every year, which is a lot for a population of five million. To break even a film needs more than 100,000 viewers. Fewer than 20 films have achieved this in the whole of the 1990s.

The money to keep the industry going comes from public funds. The national lottery Veikkaus donates about 8 million euros every year to the Finnish Film Foundation and is its main source of revenue. In 1998 the Foundation gave production support to 14 full-length motion pictures. Another source of revenue is a levy on unrecorded videocassettes. Some say that the Foundation encourages too many films, and it has certainly backed a lot of duds.

47.3. WHO ARE THE BEST FILMMAKERS?

The legendary directors of Finnish movie history had no following outside Finland. Entertaining or dull, dramatic or silly, all were cut off by walls of language and culture. Finnish motion pictures up to the 1980s either portrayed distinctly Finnish conditions or, if they attempted universal themes, were amateurish Finnish-language versions of what had been done better elsewhere.

Movies changed with a new generation of filmmakers in the 1980s, who were more interested in creativity than fame, who were therefore much more original, and who generally managed to remain within budget. These include Claes Olsson (born 1948), Veikko Aaltonen (1956) and Markku Pölönen (1957) but the top names are the Kaurismäki brothers, Mika and Aki, who have cult status abroad. No list would be complete without Renny Harlin, the one who moved to Hollywood to direct action pictures for the likes of Bruce Willis and Sylvester Stallone, and has surely had a bigger audience than all of his compatriots combined.

47.4. WHY ARE THE THEMES SO GLOOMY?

Actually they're not. The top ten Finnish films at the box office in the 1990s were a war adventure, five comedies and four romances. The minimalism of Aki Kaurismäki doesn't appeal to mass audiences at home; its bleak personalities, troubled relations and black humour are not entertaining enough. It's foreigners that have elevated this remarkable director to represent the nation.

Festivities

Easter is not big in Finland. On Palm Sunday there's a tradition of children dressing up as witches, but most adults reserve their enthusiasm for May Day, which soon follows.

The next milestone of the year is Midsummer, which has been important since pagan times, especially in the north of Europe, where seasonal differences are so great. Unlike Vappu, this is more a family or community tradition. Great bonfires are part of the occasion.

Independence Day on 6 December has ritual significance, but the greatest festivities of the year are reserved for Christmas, which has lost most of its religious force. It coincides with the darkest part of the winter, which it makes more bearable. Most of the celebrations take place on Christmas Eve.

48.1. WHAT DO I DO IF STUCK IN FINLAND DURING A RELIGIOUS HOLIDAY?

Easter Sunday may be a little quieter than other Sundays of the year but the days when all entertainment closed for religious holidays are over. As for May Day or Vappu, the biggest problem is escaping it. The centre of Helsinki has a very rowdy night and is not much fun if you're over 25. If invited to someone's home for the evening, book a taxi home early. Similarly, if you are staying outside the central area but go downtown early to see the fun, catch a ride home early before long lines start forming at taxi ranks.

Midsummer used to be a time when everyone wanted to be in the countryside but today there are plenty of events arranged for those that stay behind. The saddest season to be stuck in Helsinki alone is Christmas, when everything still gets very quiet for several days.

48.2. WHY ARE THERE SO MANY SUMMER FESTIVALS?

The Finland Festivals organization records 58 festivals arranged in Finland each summer. Most of them offer music and they draw about 1.5 million visitors. There are many in Sweden too (35 music festivals) and the trend is spreading to Norway (33 festivals). These figures list only the major events that can afford to be part of a joint marketing organization. There are lace festivals, honey festivals, even porridge festivals and of course countless events claiming to celebrate beer. The total number of Finnish summer festivals runs to many hundreds.

This is commercial exploitation of holiday tedium. Many people still want to take a full month off work in July and will try to spend a good part of it in the countryside. Even if the weather is good, most will be bored stiff after the first week and desperate for something to do. This represents an opportunity to boost rural incomes, since almost any event will attract vacationers from miles around.

48.3. WHAT ARE THE BEST FESTIVALS?

The two biggest names in music are the Savonlinna Opera Festival and Pori Jazz. Performing operas in an ancient castle was a stroke of genius that makes up for difficult acoustics, uncomfortable seating and very variable temperatures. What wine is to Savonlinna, beer is to Pori, but both promise atmosphere as much as virtuosity, and often manage to deliver both.

The big general festivals in Helsinki and Turku are

always good in parts. More specialist is the Kuhmo Chamber Music Festival. The International Mikkeli Music Festival also lives up to its name. The top rock festival is still Ruisrock in Turku. For exotic local flavour try the Kuopio Dance Festival and the Tango Festival in Seinäjoki.

48.4. WHERE SHOULD I GO FOR FOLK MUSIC?

The oldest Finnish folk music festival is Kaustinen, which dates from the 1960s. Now it is a nine-day spectacle presenting over two thousand musicians and entertaining about 100,000 people. The newer Kihaus Festival in North Karelia is smaller, lasting for four days and platforming the music of that area, plus Finno-Ugric regions across the border in Russia. Haapavesi Folk is also a small festival but features a wide range of music from the oddest corners of Europe.

The biggest folk dance event is Piispala Schottische, held in Tampere every two years. Finland's oldest festival of world folk music is Etnosoi. Held in Helsinki in October, it is the one non-summer folk event.

Design

In a culture where so much was made of wood, few early examples of Finnish design survive. Helsinki, though, is a living monument to design; the neo-classical buildings around Senate Square have been described as the world's most complete urban work of art. They were designed at the order of the Tsar of Russia by a German, C.L. Engel, in the early 19th century.

In the 20th century the Nordic countries began to apply design to consumer goods, in particular glass, ceramics and furniture. The ideal was the simplest shape compatible with a functional product that could be cheaply produced. In Finland this mirrored the functionalist movement in architecture that had replaced the national romanticism of the late 19th century.

49.1. CAN YOU EXPORT FINNISH DESIGN?

Not in a pure form. Historically, this is because designers achieved a cult status at home, where their names were used as a guarantee of quality that did not necessarily exist and had no recognition abroad. Unable to manipulate foreign markets as they had their own, Finland's artistic circles chose success by assertion, and the prefix "world-famous" was added to various prestige products that no other nation had heard of. One hallmark of Finnish design has been austerity, unappealing to foreign consumers.

In the 1970s the priests of design focussed increasingly on art products - from jewelry to wall rugs - that were immune from criticism because they served no measurable function. This reinforced the concept of design goods as expensive and elitist. But Finnish industrial designers were meanwhile pioneering concepts that would later be called ergonomics. Their work, from scissors to cruise ships, has been very successfully exported.

49.2. WHO WERE THE SAARINENS?

Eliel Saarinen was one of three ambitious architectural students who won the competition to design the Finnish pavilion at the World Exhibition in Paris in 1900. On the back of this success they went on to create some of the finest buildings in Finland. The best known is the Helsinki Railway Station. The trio also built their own home on a lake outside Helsinki, Hvitträsk, that is a place of pilgrimage today. It's all turrets and curves and fine views from cunningly placed windows. The guides spice it up with salacious tales of whiskey drinking and wife swapping.

Of the three students and partners, Saarinen is best remembered because in 1923 he decided to call it a day and move to the United States. The other Saarinen was his son, Eero, who achieved international recognition as an American architect.

49.3. WHAT WAS SPECIAL ABOUT AALTO?

Alvar Aalto (1898-1976) was the best-known Finnish architect and designer this century. He was prolific, with a range of furniture and consumer products as well as numerous buildings. He foresaw the importance of extending good design into industry, and made a good business out of it by cultivating the leading industrialists. His most famous building is the Finlandia Hall in Helsinki, which blends into the shape of the land, a mark of Aalto's technique.

He has been acclaimed as a pioneer of practical use of materials, but his skills did not meet his standards. Low maintenance costs are not a feature of his work. Finlandia Hall is faced with white Italian marble that has to be expensively replaced every twenty years because it cannot withstand Finnish winters. And the concert hall is poor: Aalto boasted that a competent architect could intuitively control functions like acoustics, and ignored the advice of engineers. Many also find his furniture awkward but, in the world of design, that is not regarded as a flaw.

49.4. SO WHY ARE THERE SO MANY UGLY BUILDINGS?

A bus journey through Finland, hopping from town centre to town centre, is depressing. Behind quaint and historic names they all look alike, identikit two-storey concrete buildings, standard supermarkets and banks, parking at the back. Old wooden towns tended to burn down at regular intervals, but their durable replacements are already dead. The same is true of many high-rise projects in the metropolitan area, the most infamous being East Pasila and Merihaka.

In the 1970s Finland was spending a massive 15-19% of its GDP on construction each year. There were no guest workers to do it on the cheap so contractors turned to industrialized construction. It has made the housing comfortable but the cityscape bleak. The banks controlled supply and demand, first financing construction and then arranging occupancy by telling customers what they could have loans for. The concept of market-oriented building is only now emerging. Demolition will be a growth business.

Nearby

Helsinki is ideally placed for visiting other parts of the Baltic. Buses leaving the station at midday are in St. Petersburg by eight in the evening, or an evening boat will get you there by the morning.

Tallinn, the capital of Estonia, is just four hours away by boat from the West Harbour or less than two hours on the frequent catamarans and hydrofoils that run, weather permitting, from the South Harbour. The granddaddy of all cruises, Helsinki to Stockholm, is done overnight on one of the giant ferries that leave the South Harbour each evening at 6 p.m. You arrive the following morning at nine.

The glorious Åland islands, Finland's finest archipelago, are a short boat ride from Turku, which is two hours by train from Helsinki. (Ferries from Helsinki to Stockholm also stop there but at 4:30 in the morning.)

50.1. WHY ISN'T ÅLAND PART OF SWEDEN?

At one time the Ålanders, who all speak Swedish, wanted to be. Lying between Finland and Sweden, Åland was part of the same kingdom as Finland and Sweden up to 1809, but was then ceded to Russia along with Finland, becoming part of the Tsar's "Grand Duchy". When Finland declared itself independent in 1917, Åland wanted to return to the Swedish fold. They mistrusted Finnish nationalism. Their unofficial parliament noted that "crude force of will is a well-known national characteristic of the Finns".

The League of Nations ruled in Finland's favour, but the islands are demilitarized by international law and have broad autonomy within Finland. They run their own police, education, health service and industrial policies. They even issue their own stamps. More importantly, they can prevent non-Ålanders from buying local property. In Sweden Åland would now be a swish colony of Stockholm. As Finns, by arrangement with the EU, they even get to keep the duty-free trade.

50.2. WHERE TO GO IN STOCKHOLM?

The Viking Line ferries that arrive each morning from Helsinki sail almost into the centre, so you can start with a walk down to the old town. Silja Line boats stop a little farther out so your day begins with a bus or metro ride.

Summer is the best time to see Stockholm but, even in the depths of winter, it's not such a bleak place as Helsinki and has a better range of shopping and museums. Stockholm also has a rich past. The Riddarholmen Church is where most Swedish rulers are buried.

From the old town you can take a ferry to Djurgården to see the remarkable Vasa Museum, devoted to a ship that sank on her maiden voyage in 1628, to be rediscovered in all her glory forty years ago. A stylish and fascinating place for lunch is the basement of the market hall at Östermalmstorg. As Sweden is not in the euro area, the price level for visitors varies with the exchange rate. To avoid hotel costs, take the same boat back in the evening, departing at 6 p.m.

50.3. WHAT TO DO IN TALLINN?

Tallinn is the perfect destination for a day cruise by rapid hydrofoil. If you come by boat you'll want to spend the night to have enough time ashore; the cheapest way is to buy a hotel package with your boat ticket. Prices are still cheap by Finnish standards but the range of goods is poor. Service is good though English is not yet widely spoken.

Concentrate your attention on the old town, a uniquely complete medieval centre preserved first by indifference and now by careful restoration. It is divided into two parts, the fortress and administrative centre above, homes and workshops for the artisans below. The square in the lower town is as close to the Middle Ages as you will ever get, and the view from upper town, Toompea, is equally magnificent. The only way around is to walk and the cobblestones are uneven. Solid shoes are a must.

50.4. HOW TO SURVIVE ST. PETERSBURG?

Tallinn, Helsinki and even Stockholm are just big towns by comparison. St. Petersburg is a metropolis with great avenues, palaces, urban sprawl, decay, pollution and crime to match. It was built on a swamp, more than 100 islands linked by 600 bridges. It's the largest port and second largest city in Russia. The Winter Palace was the official residence of the tsars and the seat of the Provisional Government during the Bolshevik revolution in 1917. Now it houses the renowned Hermitage Museum of art and antiquities. Other famous places are the great Nevsky Prospekt boulevard and the Peter and Paul Fortress, where many Russian tsars are buried.

Visas are required for travel to Russia. St. Petersburg can be reached from Helsinki by bus, train or sea. A day or even two cannot do it justice but, if that's all you've got, a cruise is the most comfortable route and also solves accommodation problems because you sleep safely on your ship.

T

take-home pay · 103
Tallinn · 144, 205, 207
Taloussanomat · 152
Tampere · 118, 125, 150, 183, 200
tango · 165
tar · 112, 139
taxation · 89
taxi drivers · 167
teacher's pay · 103
team sports · 158
technology · 125, 148
tele-cluster · 124
telecom operators · 145
telecommunications · 127
telecommunications equipment · 121
telecommuting · 100
telegraph · 146
telephones · 145
television · 153
Telia · 146
tennis · 160
tenting · 178
theft · 53
thunder · 19
time zone · 14
tipping · 166
tobacco · 56, 154
toilets · 168
Toompea · 208
Torvalds, Linus · 148
touring · 177
track and field · 157
tractors · 116
trade · 93
trade press · 153
trading partners · 94
trains · 141
transformers · 121
transport · 97, 100, 141

trees · 25, 109
trekking · 177
trotting · 160
trout · 173
trucks · 116
True Finns · 73
tundra · 15
Turku · 19, 115, 150, 177, 180, 186
tv · 149
tv news · 150
tv sets · 95

U

Ukko · 186
unemployment · 51, 102, 128
unemployment benefit · 51
United Nations · 77, 80
universities · 45, 128, 147
university · 47, 128
Uralic people · 38
Utsjoki · 21
Uusi Suomi · 150

W

waiter's pay · 102
Valio · 156
Waltari, Mika · 193
waltz · 165
Vantaa · 33, 143
WAP · 136
Vappu · 197
Vasa Museum · 207
VAT · 92, 98
Vatanen, Ari · 159
waterfowl · 173
wave power · 139
weasel · 29
weather · 17
web surfing · 124

The outside world is increasingly interested in Finland, its environment, economy and technology. "Finland in a Small Book" tackles the issues that foreigners are really curious about, not necessarily what Finns would expect them to ask or would like to tell them.

The design – two hundred frequently asked questions on a great array of subjects – makes it easy for the reader to find exactly what he needs. Some matters are inevitably controversial but never dull.

ABOUT THE AUTHOR

Patrick Humphreys, a British-born economist and journalist, worked in Finland in the 1980s and 1990s as a news editor for the Finnish Broadcasting Company and then as Reuters' correspondent.

His other books about economy and ecology include Forests in Global Warming, Harmony of Life and Nature and the annual Yearbooks of the Finnish Economy.

He is currently the Secretary General of the 24-nation Association of European Journalists.